W9-ACJ-770

Sisters in Arms

A Father Remembers

John Witmer

Library Lane Publishing

www.librarylanepublishing.com

Request for information should be addressed to:

Library Lane Publishing, 15263 Library Lane, New Berlin WI 53151

Copyright © John Witmer 2010

Printed in the United States of America

Library of Congress Cataloging-in-Publication Data

Witmer, John

Sisters in Arms : A Father Remembers/John Witmer – 1st Ed

ISBN 978-0-9845804-0-8

LCCN: 2010907419

Sisters in Arms is a memoir and the events described within are what the author remembers to the best of his ability.

CONTENTS

Prologue...vii

Chapter 1 – Up on My Roof 1

Chapter 2 – Don't Drop that Baby................................ 5

Chapter 3 – Lost in the Woods 13

Chapter 4 – Exile.. 17

Chapter 5 – Wars and Rumors of Wars..................... 23

Chapter 6 – Like Sands through the Hour Glass........ 29

Chapter 7 – Strangers in a Strange Land 35

Chapter 8 – Then There Were Three......................... 51

Chapter 9 – Fifteen Days 55

Chapter 10 – The End in Sight 61

Chapter 11 – The Knock... 65

Chapter 12 – Holy Saturday...................................... 71

Chapter 13 – In the Spotlight 77

Chapter 14 – Directive 1315.7................................. 85

Chapter 15 – Angels of Mercy 91

Chapter 16 – Sleepwalking 97

Chapter 17 – Casualties of War................................ 109

Chapter 18 – The Crush of the Crowd 113

Chapter 19 – The 32nd Returns 119

Chapter 20 – The Spotlight Fades............................. 123

Chapter 21 – Picking up the Pieces 129

Chapter 22 – Sister Nirmala 139

Chapter 23 – Five 143

Chapter 24 – A Rose in the Desert 151

Chapter 25 – The Homecoming 155

Chapter 26 – Dear Dad 159

Epilogue – A Letter to Madison 161

For Michelle and Madison with thanks and appreciation to my wife, Lori, who encouraged me to start this journey and to Rachel, Charity, Tim and Mark who encouraged me to finish it.

Prologue

Raising five children has been the greatest adventure of my life, yet, when I started this journey, I never dreamed it would bring me to a day where I would say goodbye to all three of my daughters as they marched off to war—not as part of a women's auxiliary, but as part of a fully-trained, fully-equipped fighting force. There was no fanfare to mark this change in the way the U.S. military operated; it came quietly, born of necessity. As America's military struggles to recruit the soldiers it needs, America's daughters have stepped in to the gap, training alongside our sons and taking their place among the troops. Yes, women are still barred from the infantry and other "frontline" roles, but these rules have little effect in wars without frontlines, like those we are fighting in Iraq and Afghanistan. Just like their male counterparts our women are frequently under enemy attack and like their male counterparts they return fire with their M-16s or their turret-mounted machine guns.

In 2005, the House Armed Services Committee held hearings on the role of women in the Military. It was prompted by rising female casualties. At that time over 35 women had been killed in action in the Iraq and Afghanistan wars and another 260 had been wounded. There was some brief grandstanding on the part of some committee members expressing their concern and proposing legislation designed to make sure female soldiers would be removed from harm's way. But the controversy quickly dropped out of the news. I suspect it was the result of some four-star General giving the Representatives this simple math lesson: one in seven of the 150,000 troops stationed in Iraq at the time were female. Removing all of them from hostile fire zones would have crippled Operation Iraqi Freedom.

This book is not a political statement; it is simply my story, a father's story about sending children off to war and waiting for them to come home and what it's like when they don't come home.

Chapter 1 - Up on My Roof

Baghdad, Iraq, 2003

Rachel and her squad took their positions on the roof of the battered concrete building that served as the neighborhood police station. In recent weeks, insurgents had focused their assaults on these fragile beacons of law and order. In this war without frontlines, the 32nd MPs were given the task of providing security for the Iraqi Police, so attacks on police stations were both an attack on the post-Saddam regime and the U.S. government. Police stations were a convenient and efficient target.

The sun was low and the day-shift convoy had just pulled out heading back to Camp Victory after their twelve-hour watch. The police station, in Al Adamia, was just large enough to house a few cells and some dingy offices. It was far from inviting, and Rachel never completely trusted the IPs (Iraqi Police) she worked with; if she found herself in the unfortunate circumstance of needing to use the dilapidated commode, she kept her sidearm ready.

She began her routine, setting up her M-16 and scanning the streets below in slow, rhythmic sweeps, watching for anything that seemed out of place: a truck moving a little too slowly, a pedestrian moving a little too quickly, or a moment that was just a little too quiet. In the months that preceded this one, Rachel and her team had taken small arms fire and mortar fire and had dealt with their share of grenades. She was just a few minutes into her watch when she heard it, a sound she couldn't place. It was like the sound of the surf in the distance.

Rachel struggled to understand where the sound was coming from. Her apprehension grew as she attempted to find an explanation. Her eyes carefully traced the streets below until she saw it; a wave of humanity, off in the distance, making its way toward the station. Not the roar of the ocean, the roar of the crowd, an angry, roiling, gun-waving mob.

Now she could make out the voice of the mullah (a religious leader) crackling over a loudspeaker. The rapid-fire words seemed to be urging the crowd on. Rachel could only imagine what was being said, but the words erupted from the primitive speaker with anger. The streets of Iraq traded in rumor and conspiracy, and this uprising could have been sparked by any one of the wild stories that routinely circulated about American soldiers: that they desecrated mosques, molested children, or spread pornography. It was clear that the gun-waving mob was heading their direction, hell-bent on taking revenge on this handful of soldiers, the most visible manifestation of the American military. The sergeant radioed the day shift and told them to double-time it back to the police station. Rachel was grateful for the reinforcements, but still, there was no way they could fend off an armed mob of this size.

As Rachel took her stand on the roof, time began to expand, seconds passing like minutes, altered by the adrenaline that now pumped into her bloodstream. In that heightened state of awareness, in a moment of clarity, Rachel accepted the fact that it might end here, that this might be her last stand, her last day on Earth. As she prepared herself, she was suddenly calm. Peace came over her as she reflected on the people she cared about, bringing their faces to mind, one-by-one, as the pounding of her heart subsided.

Her sisters came to mind first. Michelle served with her in the 32nd MPs. Michelle's platoon was pulling the same kind of duty in a different part of Baghdad. Then Charity: she was a medic with the Company B 118th Medical Battalion, stationed at BIAP, Baghdad International Airport, on the other side of town. She brought her brothers' faces to mind, little brother Tim, just two years younger, and baby brother Mark, now a senior in high school. Then she thought about Mom and Dad and aunts and uncles and dozens of cousins. She wondered what it would be like for them if it all came to an end, here, on this rooftop in Baghdad.

This was not the first time Rachel had experienced this: time standing still, recalling the faces of those she loved, making peace with death, bracing herself. There had been a mortar attack on her barracks, in the middle of the night, that had shaken her awake. As she lay on the floor calculating how long it would take the insurgents to dial in the next strike, which would likely be dead-on target, this same sensation came over her. Fear left her; she was resolute, ready to accept her fate. Then the choppers came in and she heard the report of a big gun and she knew the insurgents would not fire another round. The threat had been neutralized. The chopper hovered, standing watch over the barracks, and the sound of helicopter blades sang Rachel to sleep that night.

A new noise pulled her back into real time: the unmistakable thudding of helicopter blades. The Blackhawk hovered above the crowd, and all forward motion stopped as its guns were trained on the throng below. The mob continued to shout and wave their weapons, but now tanks were rolling up the side streets, blocking the way to the police station. The standoff continued as the sun inched toward the horizon. But slowly and steadily the crowd thinned, melting into the twilight.

Waukesha, Wisconsin, 2000

The recruiter hit the jackpot, a two-for-one special. Rachel and Charity sat at his desk looking at pamphlets. He explained that, yes, Charity could sign-up when she turned seventeen, as long as she had her parents' permission and a high school diploma. The sign-on on bonus? $8000, half after basic-training and half after finishing three years of the six-year contract. "And don't forget the GI Bill," he reminded. All they had to do was pick one of the bonus-eligible MOSs (Military Occupational Specialty) and military police or medical specialist both qualified.

It was the fall of 2000. Rachel was two years out of high school. She had worked at various jobs but hadn't quite settled on a direction in life. She was well-read and intelligent, but the last few years of high school had been a grind, and she wasn't ready to jump back into the books. But when she *was* ready to go to college, she wanted to do it on her own. If she asked for Mom and Dad to help with the expenses, there would be strings attached. She was supporting herself and she wanted it to stay that way. Joining the Guard seemed to be the answer: a bonus, job training, and money for school. She signed on the dotted line as sixteen-year old Charity looked on with envy.

In January 2001, we stood with Rachel as she checked in to a hotel across the street from Milwaukee's MEPS – military speak for "Military Entrance Processing Station." MEPS would be the first of hundreds of new acronyms Rachel would learn over the next four months. In the morning, she would receive a wake-up call at 4:00 a.m. and the induction process would begin; the day would be full of medical tests and examinations. Then, late the next day, she would board a bus to Milwaukee's Billy Mitchell Field. A plane would take her to St Louis and another bus ride would land her at her destination:

Fort Leonard Wood, Missouri, one of the toughest basic training facilities in the country.

She had to be in her room and accounted for by 10:00 p.m. We lingered in the hotel lobby until the last minute, the whole clan: Mom (Lori), Dad, Tim, Michelle, Charity, and Mark, making small talk. "We'll be there for graduation; write us and tell us when it is just as soon as you find out," Lori reminded her again. We had always been a close-knit family, and saying goodbye, even for four months, was difficult.

Two days later, Rachel was moving through a line at Fort Leonard Wood, Missouri, collecting her gear as the drill sergeants screamed instructions to the new recruits. Finding combat boots in a size four had not been easy, but the gear was collected in a duffel bag. She wrote us describing carrying her duffle bag full of her new gear: "We had to hold the duffle bag in front of us as we walked. It was almost as tall as I was and weighed nearly as much." From the beginning, it was clear that the drill sergeants meant to tear the recruits down so that they could then be reassembled into soldiers. Many in this group would not make it. "A lot of recruits have washed out," she wrote a few weeks later, "we're down to 280 from about 320. One of the guys attempted suicide last night."

I marveled at Rachel's tenacity as I read her boot camp letters. It wasn't just that she endured the long days or the relentless physical training; she made it through the mind games. "For now, we're only allowed to eat with a spoon. When we get into the next phase, the drill sergeants may let us have a fork." Through it all, she remained positive, and when we saw her again, at her graduation, there was no doubt that my first-born daughter had become a soldier.

Chapter 2 - Don't Drop that Baby

Oconomowoc, Wisconsin, 1984

Rachel was busy with her Fisher-Price tea set in the bedroom with bright blue-and-green striped carpeting that she shared with her brother Timothy. She was four years old, old enough to sleep on the top bunk and old enough to stay out of the way while her mom was in labor. Timothy was only two, too young to understand and too young to occupy himself, so he had been sent to stay with friends.

In the next room, Rachel's mother, Lori, had just given birth to a healthy baby girl. "I told you I gained too much weight!" Lori fretted over the size of her stomach as she held her new daughter tightly in her arms. "Can we name her Michelle?" Lori and I had gone back and forth. She favored "Michelle Marie," and I liked "Charity Gail". Oddly, neither of us could come up with a boy's name, so we were relieved not to be dealing with that decision.

Michelle Witmer came into this world in the bedroom of our apartment above the carriage house—the caretaker's quarters. I cut grass and plowed snow on an eight-acre estate, situated on a beautiful lake near Oconomowoc, Wisconsin, in exchange for use of the caretaker's apartment. The mansion that used to grace the estate had been taken in a fire decades earlier, and a sprawling ranch home with a large pool and an incredible view of the lake had replaced it. The carriage house, built during the early 1900s was situated on the far edge of the property, nestled between pine trees on one side and a corn field on the other. The view from the south windows was picturesque: big trees crowding the rolling grounds. The view from the north windows, the side the bedrooms were on, was an enormous farm field, with the remains of golden corn stalks stretching out as far as the eye could see.

Only a cold-hearted man could watch his wife go through labor and then veto her choice for the baby's name. Lori was just 25. It was her third pregnancy and her third home delivery. So, "yes," we would name the baby Michelle Marie, and I hurried to the phone to let my mother know that her newest grandchild would share her birthday: February 13th.

In 1984, the year Michelle was born, I marked seven years as a member of small, fundamentalist church that had at the center of its theology the incompatibility of medical science and "true faith." Over the years, the shunning of medical science evolved from a recommended practice to an absolute requirement for anyone expecting to find eternal salvation. That's why Michelle was born in our bedroom with no doctor in attendance. This was our third pregnancy, and by now, it felt routine.

Mrs. C., a woman who had cared for other church families during home deliveries, had come by to assist us in whatever way she could. She remarked that Lori was still having nice, strong contractions and encouraged her to work with them to expedite the delivery of the afterbirth. She suggested that the contractions might be more productive if she got up and moved around; if she tried laboring in different positions.

And that's how Michelle's twin sister came to be born on the bathroom floor; on that small piece of real estate between the sink and the bathtub. She was the best surprise of our lives. If Charity Gail would have opened her little eyes, she would have seen her parents, dumfounded, staring back at her. Lori was lying on the floor, a look of wonder on her face. I clutched Charity's slippery body, cradling her head and hanging on to her feet, lacing them in my fingers. Mrs. C. ran around looking for something to wrap her in and something to use to tie off the umbilical cord while shouting, "Don't drop that baby!"

We had taken great care in preparing for Michelle. Her blankets were gently warmed in the oven. A mail-order birthing kit, including a fancy plastic cord clamp, was carefully staged on a sterile pad. A tiny stocking cap waited to keep her head warm.

Charity got wrapped in a towel, capped with an odd sock, and tied off with a piece of yarn. She may have been the second twin out of the womb, but it seemed, in that moment, Charity determined it would be the last time she ever came in second.

New Berlin, Wisconsin, 2000

Charity was in the first semester of her junior year and she was miserable, "I hate it! She reminded us on a daily basis. She and Michelle had transferred from Waukesha West after we made the decision to move to a larger house in New Berlin, Wisconsin, located in the Brookfield Central School District. Going in, it looked like no big deal. Their new high school was less than ten miles from their old one. They could stay in contact with their old friends while meeting new people at their new school. But a few weeks into the school year, it became clear that the switch was a problem. Charity and Michelle were outsiders, and some of the girls in the established cliques wanted to make sure they remained outsiders. It all came to a head when we got word that the twins were routinely skipping school.

"You'll have to take the bus to school; I'm taking away your car," I informed Charity.

"It's my car!" Charity shouted back. And she was technically correct. She had purchased the little two-door Chrysler with money she earned waiting tables, saving up enough cash for the purchase, by her sixteenth birthday.

"But until you're eighteen, you can only drive it if I give you permission," I responded, doing my best impersonation of a trial lawyer. "You'll take the bus to school for the next two weeks, and if you continue to skip school, you won't get the car back."

Lori and I met with Michelle and Charity's high school counselor, trying to get some insight into the reason our girls were so miserable. We fully expected to be told that Michelle and Charity were exaggerating about the social situation and that all they needed to do was give it some more time. Instead the counselor seemed to confirm what we had been told, using the word "vicious" when describing the school's systems of cliques.

Charity and Michelle were not your average high school kids; they were street smart. We had home-schooled them at various times in their lives, and they knew full-well that there were many paths to a high school diploma, paths that didn't involve cliques and catty classmates. They formulated a plan and then sat us down to explain it. Charity took the lead while Michelle covered her flank: "We want you to hear us out before you say anything," and with that they produced papers containing their school transcripts and began to elaborate. "We want to leave Brookfield Central and enroll in Christian Liberty Academy." CLA, based in Chicago, had a "satellite program;" in effect it was a correspondence school.

"We have enough credits to enroll as seniors," Charity continued. "Yeah, Mom, all those years you made us go to summer school were good for something after all," Michelle added.

Charity got right back on point, "If we work hard, we can complete the coursework by spring and graduate a year early. Then we want to join the National Guard." Michelle nodded in agreement. "If you give your permission, we can sign up when we turn seventeen, next February."

"Look what the Guard has done for Rachel," Michelle added, referring to the confident demeanor Rachel had adopted since returning from boot camp.

"And if you send us back to Brookfield Central, we're all going to be miserable." Charity's statement seemed to contain a veiled threat.

Lori and I left the room to talk it over. We were stunned, but at the same time, proud. It seemed, in that moment, our twins had graduated from rebellious teenagers to responsible adults. We knew our girls, and we knew they were serious. We returned to the kitchen, and after laying out all the caveats and disclaimers, we let them know we would sign-on to their plan and support them as long as they could show consistent progress toward graduation.

The whole mood of the house changed. Instead of being at war with our teenagers, we had become allies with the responsible young adults they had become. Charity graduated in spring, and Michelle graduated a few months later, and when they asked us to, we signed the papers giving consent for our seventeen-year-old daughters to enlist in the National Guard.

Charity began attending drills shortly after she signed on in the spring of 2001. But she was not scheduled to leave for basic training until September. Charity reminded Rachel, often, that she would be receiving basic training in Fort Jackson, South Carolina, not in Fort Leonard Wood. "Relaxin' in Jackson" Charity taunted. Compared to Fort Leonard Wood's program, Fort Jackson was supposed to be a walk in the park.

I remember standing in the kitchen that September, watching wall-to-wall news coverage of the 9/11 terrorist attacks. Charity was supposed to leave on September 13th, but now the whole world was upside down and I wondered how these events would affect her. I remember a knot forming in my stomach as I realized that my daughters were now serving in the military in a time of war.

All commercial flights had been grounded and the Army was scrambling to find transportation for its recruits. As a result, Charity was rerouted to Fort Leonard Wood for basic training. She would be bused to Missouri to go through the same, arduous program Rachel went through. After all the grief she had given Rachel, the change of plans would have been funny had the circumstances that caused them been different.

Charity finished her "91 whiskey" (combat medic) training in April 2002, and that summer the Company B 118th was sent to Nicaragua on a "compassionate mission." They flew into Managua and then convoyed out to the countryside on what passed for roads; in reality they were two ruts in the mud. They crawled to their remote base where they provided medical attention to the poorest of the poor. It was a life-changing experience for Charity, and when she returned to the States, she shared her stories with anyone who would listen.

"There's this family that lives just outside the compound," she explained. "Three generations live together, and the grandparents, parents, and children all make their living by taking big rocks and breaking them up into gravel. The money they make is barely enough to feed them all, but they have a dream that keeps them going. They want to save enough money to pay for school for the youngest girl." She told of a mob of young boys who clamored, just outside the gate, for the chance to earn a few cents shining the soldiers' shoes. And she watched as the boy she paid, handsomely, to shine her boots ended up surrendering the money to an older boy who threaten to beat him.

"There was a man who came to the camp after walking for days," she told us. "His foot was badly injured and infected, and by the time he got to us, it needed to be amputated." This was just one of many cases where the lack of medical attention transformed simple illnesses into fatal conditions. Her passion for the people of Nicaragua was so strong she considered returning, a feat that could only be accomplished by transferring to the Ohio National Guard. All this took place before her eighteenth birthday.

If Charity couldn't wait to grow up, she probably caught the condition from her older brother, Timothy. Besides being in a hurry to reach adulthood, Timothy was a risk-taker. He was fascinated by chemistry, and he was adept at navigating the Internet long before most people knew what the Internet was. At a very early age, he pulled stunts like blowing up plastic Coke bottles in our front yard by combining common household chemicals he had learned about online.

He liked to do everything fast, and this continued once he started driving; he racked up speeding tickets, barely hanging on to his driver's license. He was good with his hands; he and a friend would often spend hours in the garage working on their cars, installing mega-sound systems with huge subwoofers that would shake the entire neighborhood.

School was so easy for Tim that he found it boring. He received his high-school diploma from Waukesha West, a school he rarely attended. He transferred in as a junior after the financial burden of private school became too much for the family, but he spent most of that year taking courses at the local community college, showing up at West High School only for the required gym and health classes. He skipped his senior year after his application for early graduation was approved.

At seventeen, Tim worked evenings at the local hospital where he was supposed to be doing clerical work for the lab. But he soon figured out how to automate most of his job, which consisted of taking data from one hospital system and re-keying it into another, so he had several free hours each night to learn other skills. He used the time to study up on the hospital computer systems, networks, and lab equipment, knowledge he leveraged into a career by the time he turned twenty-one.

He moved to the East Side of Milwaukee to attend the University of Wisconsin–Milwaukee, taking a break, in the winter of 2001 to backpack around Europe for several months, telling us, only after he returned, that he had left the States with less than two hundred dollars in his pocket. He stayed in youth hostels and worked for cash, doing a stint as a waiter at a Greek restaurant in London. After he returned from Europe, Tim remained close to his siblings, often sharing his East Side apartment with them as they studied together at the university.

Michelle finished high school in what would have been the summer before her senior year. She was impressed by the changes she had seen in Rachel: the maturity, the commitment, the patriotism. She had listened with great interest to the stories Charity brought back with her from Nicaragua and noted the deep impression the mission had made on her. So in early 2002, Michelle went to see the same recruiter Rachel and Charity had worked with.

Unlike Charity, who got her driver's license the day she turned sixteen, Michelle had never been in a hurry to drive, and it had never been a problem, since her twin sister was willing to take her wherever she needed to go. "I've got to have my driver's license to get into the Guard," she explained. "The recruiter said I can sign up, but I have to pass my driver's exam before I leave for basic training." She was scheduled to leave for boot camp shortly after her 18th birthday. She signed up for a compressed driving course, drove the required number of supervised practice hours, and went to take her driver's test just a few weeks before she was scheduled to leave.

"I didn't pass!" Michelle reported with desperation in her voice as she returned to the exam station. She was devastated. She didn't know it then, but she would go on to drive Humvees through some of the most harrowing traffic in the world, and she would, one day, be praised for getting her commander to his meeting on time by driving on Baghdad sidewalks and medians. But all this would have to wait until she mastered parallel parking.

Mark, Michelle's younger brother, studied alongside her as she finished up her high school courses. Mark had also opted for home-school as a way to devote more time to his gymnastics career. He had begun competing when he was eight years old and had qualified for "Nationals" every year since becoming a teenager. College scholarships were scarce for men's gymnastics, but Mark's dedication was likely to earn him a spot on a Big-Ten team. He would also follow in his siblings' footsteps, graduating a full year early.

Chapter 3 - Lost in the Woods

Fort Leonard Wood, Missouri, 2002

It is 501 miles from New Berlin, Wisconsin, to Fort Leonard Wood, Missouri, a journey we had made twice before for Rachel and Charity's boot camp graduations. The 16,000 soldiers who passed though the training center every year had dubbed it "Fort Leonard Wood, Misery" or "Fort Lost in the Woods." Leonard Wood had served as Army Chief of Staff in 1910, under President Taft; now Michelle was graduating from boot camp at the Army base that bore his name, and we were, once again, traveling through the dense green country side of Missouri through the long stretches of rolling highway between St. Louis and Fort Leonard Wood.

We had done this enough times to know what to expect: hundreds of recruits, from all over the country, from every social stratum, from every race and creed, and the families to which they belonged. I had learned to arrive early. If the graduation ceremony was scheduled for two in the afternoon, the cars, RVs, and campers would start rolling through the front gates early in the morning, as soon as the guards would let them through. Families stood in line at the auditorium hours before the doors opened and then rushed to claim seats as soon as they were let inside. Then they would sit, patiently, for another ninety minutes waiting for the ceremony began.

The letters would arrive on Army provided stationary: half-sized sheets with the Army insignia at the top and light ruling in the background to facilitate handwritten letters. They were written somewhere between 8:30 p.m., when free time began, and lights out, which occurred promptly at 9:30 p.m. A common theme was describing training activities that boggled the mind of the civilian reader. Michelle wrote, "In the past week, I've done about a zillion things including a road march, gas chamber, warrior tower (A.K.A.: the tree house from hell) and I'm learning a ton. The gas chamber sucked, but it certainly cleared my sinuses."

And, of course, there were the descriptions of the drill sergeants.

I have three platoon drill sergeants. Two of them are evil, the third, D.S. Smith is Satan himself. He talks like a rabid grizzly with a southern accent. Oh, yeah, those comics Rae sent me, I never got to read them because D.S. Smith crumpled them up when I opened the letter. ... Today is Easter and I'm very exhausted. I only got three hours of sleep last night 'cause of the time change and fire guard. Nothing special at all has happened except for a church service. They still yell and scream today. Well, only one more week of this 'til white phase.

Basic training was divided into three phases, red, white, and blue. Red phase is designed to break down the civilian recruit in preparation for rebuilding as a soldier, white phase introduces the recruits to the use of weapons, and blue phase puts all the training together in battlefield exercises.

I have this drill Sergeant who has made me his special project," Michelle wrote. "Yesterday he was screaming at me for about the hundredth time that day and it really started to get to me and I guess it showed. He yells, '*Do I scare you Witmer!*' and before I could think about it, I shouted back, '*Yes, Drill Sergeant, you scare the shit out of me, Drill Sergeant.*' He looked at me like he couldn't believe what had just come out of my mouth, and I braced myself for what was coming next. Instead, he got real quiet, and with his thick southern accent he said, 'Well, at least my *dog* likes me' and he walked away.

Sometimes I wake up in the morning at O'dark-thirty o'clock and I'm like 'Hey Michelle Witmer, you're in Missouri. What the heck were you thinking!?' I'm just taking it day-by-day and I'm focusing on the light at the end of the tunnel: graduation.

Like her sisters before her, Michelle made it through boot camp, and now we sat waiting in the auditorium for her graduation ceremony. When the soldiers finally began to file in, every neck craned, as family members began searching for the face of their loved one. Some couldn't hold back, and when they spotted their son or daughter, they began waving and calling out their name. But their soldier would not break step or turn to look, precisely because they were soldiers now.

When we lined up to get into the ceremony, we were near the back of the line, and when we finally got into the auditorium, it was hard to find six seats together. One of us covered some seats while the others scouted for better ones. There were open seats in the very front, but they were roped off for special guests. We retreated to the best seats we could find and the ceremony began.

The ceremonies were always moving, but in this particular program, we were shocked and delighted to discover that the award for "Soldier of the Cycle" was going to our Michelle. Afterward, when we went forward to congratulate her, we noticed the seats in the front of the auditorium that had been roped off. A sign hung from the rope that said "Reserved for the family of Michelle Witmer."

Chapter 4 - Exile

San Antonio, Texas, 1985

Rachel was nearly five years old when we moved to Texas. To that point in her life, she had never seen a doctor or dentist; she had never worn a pair of pants or listened to popular music. The only time she had been exposed to television was on the occasional visit to a relative's house. She had never celebrated Christmas or any other holiday except Thanksgiving, and she had been raised by parents who saw corporal punishment as a scriptural mandate.

Lori and I met in church, and our fervent desire to find and follow God's will was what first brought us together. We were very young when we got married: Lori was twenty and I was twenty-one. In obedience to the scriptural mandate to "be fruitful and multiply," Rachel was born before Lori's twenty-first birthday. Our spiritual journey would shape the lives of our children. They would watch as, over the years, as we moved away from the extreme doctrines of the little storefront church where Lori and I had met to the mainstream teachings of Christianity, changing churches more than half-dozen times along the way. And though our beliefs moderated considerably over the years, our emphasis on faith and family remained constant.

Lori and I believed that it was up to us to educate our children in a way that reflected our core values. Sometimes we could accomplish this through the public school systems and sometimes we had to find other ways. Over the years, this meant the children rotated between public, private, and home-based education. We would make whatever adjustments necessary to keep them on track, and we always supplement their education with Sunday school and week-night church programs.

The twins had just turned one when we began our self-imposed exile in Texas. We left Wisconsin after a dramatic falling out with the church we had attended for seven years, and we were looking for a fresh start. Charity and Michelle celebrated their birthday by getting the chicken pox, a gift they gladly shared with Rachel and Timothy. The miniature epidemic set the tone for our first year in San Antonio, one of the hardest years of lives.

We didn't know a soul. My sister Anna lived a couple hours north, in Austin, but we saw her only occasionally. Living rent free, as we did when I was caretaking in Wisconsin, we were insulated from the rising cost of housing. As it turned out, the increase in salary, which came with my new job, barely covered our new expenses; there would be no extra money. I went to work early and came home late, which meant Lori spent long, lonely days taking care of our four, soon to be five, children; Lori became pregnant with Mark shortly after we moved to San Antonio.

Lori was a devoted mother. She read to the kids, played with them, sang to them, cooked for them, sewed clothes for them, and taught them. Rachel turned six while we lived in San Antonio, and Lori selected a home-school curriculum and began Rachel's formal education. She found it easier to keep four-year-old Timothy occupied by including him in the first-grade lessons. She was pregnant, with four small children, home-schooling two of them, and babysitting another child to supplement our income, and she seemed to take it all in stride.

Rachel, Tim, Michelle, and Charity had no idea that we were struggling financially. There was always food on the table. They thought it was great that sometimes they got to have pancakes for both breakfast *and* supper. And library cards work regardless of whether you have money in your checking account, a fact we exploited. The kids were thrilled to get the second-hand toys, bicycles, and tricycles we bought for next to nothing at yard sales, and it was amazing to see how much fun they could have with a five-dollar wading pool and a garden hose. They spent afternoons playing on the old swing set I hauled into the back yard after buying it for a few bucks from a neighbor. And when it was time to go to church, their Sunday best was as nice as any of the other children. The matching dresses Lori made for the girls always made them the center of attention.

My affinity for computers earned me an interview with my company's engineering group. But the interview ended abruptly when it came out that I did not have a degree, a fact the manager who hired me chose to keep under wraps. In the weeks that followed, I was asked to provide documentation for the programs I had written, and it became clear that the company was preparing to fire me.

I used what little vacation time I had to travel back to Wisconsin for job interviews. The goal was to find a job in Milwaukee and move back "home." I asked a former co-worker if I could use his name as a reference. He mentioned this in passing to my former boss, who, in turn, contacted me about a position, he was trying to fill. The offer was more than I had hoped for and it included relocation. The only problem was the job was not in Wisconsin, it was in Chaska, Minnesota.

As we wrestled with whether or not to accept the offer, my boss informed me that if I didn't resign by the end of the month, I would be fired. The ultimatum brought clarity to the situation. Chaska was about 350 miles from Milwaukee, a reasonable weekend drive. I would have a job with a company I knew, working for I man I respected. I could not afford to be unemployed, not even for a little while. We reasoned we could try again, in a couple of years, to move back to Wisconsin.

Our years in Minnesota were some of the happiest in our lives. As the kids grew older, Lori began working outside the home, eventually taking a wait staff position at the Chanhassen Dinner Theaters. It was Lori's connection to the dinner theaters that resulted in Rachel being granted an audition for *The Music Man*. Rachel now ten-years old, belted out an audition song and landed a spot in the chorus, singing and dancing for 180 shows. Tim followed Rachel on to the stage, landing a part in *Peter Pan* at the Minneapolis Children's Theater.

Lori was almost fanatical about making certain our children were constructively occupied. TV time continued to be rationed, and the kids were encouraged to be involved and active. She logged hundreds of miles every week taking Rachel, Charity, and Michelle to dance class and hundreds more taking all the children to auditions or rehearsals. Rachel and Tim added TV commercials and voice-over work to their resumes, lending their voices to an educational track for the Minneapolis Planetarium and to a series of children's tapes called *G.T. and the Halo Express*.

We lived in Minnesota for nearly seven years, and we were as happy as we had ever been, but in 1993, tragedy struck the company I worked for. The V.P. of operations, the man who had hired me into the company, the man I considered my mentor, died suddenly of a massive heart attack. There was no warning; he died at the office. He was only fifty-four years old. Several weeks later, I was asked to move to the company's corporate headquarters in New Berlin, Wisconsin, to fill the vacancy left by his untimely death.

It was one of the most difficult decisions we ever had to make. We loved living in Minnesota. We had been blessed with many close friends, and we found a church that seemed to work for the whole family. Moving meant starting over again in so many ways. I took the job, but I second-guessed the decision for years as I watched the family adjust to new schools, a new church, and a new neighborhood.

Rachel was thirteen when we made our third and final cross-country move to Waukesha, Wisconsin; Tim was eleven, the twins were nine, and Mark was seven. Wisconsin is where our children would come of age, where they would experience all the typical teenage rites of passage: proms and plays, first cars and first accidents, dates and curfews, curfew violations and groundings, and arguments ending in those classic words, "You're so *unfair!*", inevitably followed by the slamming of a bedroom door.

In those years, Lori continued her commitment to making sure our children were constructively occupied. "Too much free time was an invitation for trouble," she would say, "especially unsupervised free time." She chauffeured the kids to cross-country meets, soccer matches, and baseball games. She spent countless hours on the bleachers, watching our daughters cheerleading, watching our son's gymnastics meets or waiting, for one of our clan to come across the finish line at a cross-country meet.

In 1994, Lori met another mother who shared her busy-hands-are-happy-hands philosophy. Fran Teskie and her husband Neil operated a fishery and an orchard in Door County, a picturesque resort area about four hours north of Milwaukee. They had a store where they sold what they had grown or caught: apples, cherries, strawberries, blackberries, and, of course, whitefish. Whitefish boils were a Door County tradition, and the Teskie's commercial fishing operation was one of the primary sources of the whitefish so coveted by Door County tourists. They rounded out the store's offerings with gourmet cheeses, preserves, and baked goods. They had seven children who, like their parents, had learned to work long hours in the fields, on the boat, or in the store.

When Fran shared with Lori that she was struggling to find enough summer help, Lori suggested that thirteen-year-old Timothy could spend the summer with the Teskies and lend a hand. Eventually, every one of our children would spend summers with the Teskies working in Door County, an experience that would shape their lives. Mrs. Teskie insisted that everyone who boarded in the enormous farmhouse get up early and start their day with devotions. Then it was out to the fields to pick strawberries, back to the house for chores, over to the dock to help clean fish, half an hour for a quick swim in Lake Michigan, then on to weeding or mowing or working in the store. They spent hours working alongside Mrs. Teskie, and over the years she became a second mother to them.

The effect of learning to work, early in life, seemed to result in a general impatience with the traditional education process. Rachel was the only one of our children to endure four years of high school and a cap-and-gown-graduation. Tim, Charity, Michelle, and Mark all found ways to graduate early, with little fanfare. All our children seemed to be eager to leave high school behind and make their way in life, and for our girls, that path led to the Wisconsin National Guard.

Chapter 5 - Wars and Rumors of Wars

A soldier's parent listens to the news differently than the general population. Operation Enduring Freedom began in October of 2001 with the invasion of Afghanistan. The stated goal was to capture Osama Bin Laden and remove the Taliban from power. As U.S. troops were deployed to Afghanistan, we were left to wonder what role reservists might play in the war effort. I naively believed that, although my daughters might be called up, they would be assigned duties stateside, filling in behind an active duty soldier who had been deployed overseas. In the year that followed, I began to hear about National Guard units being deployed overseas. Charity, in the middle of her Christmas letter, put words to our unspoken fears.

> Rachel, Tim, Michelle, and I are all attending college at UWM, this semester, with Rachel majoring in music, Tim in computer science, Michelle in broadcast journalism and myself in nursing. … Rachel, Michelle, and I have been watching the news intently and hoping that we will not be deployed any time soon. We will keep you all updated.

She went on to describe little brother Mark's gymnastics schedule and his newfound interest in acoustic guitar, sandwiching the jarring words about the possibility of deployment between casual updates, as if by doing so, she could make us forget about the elephant in the room: that it was likely that they were going to war.

Only a few weeks later, all doubt was gone; Rachel and Michelle received orders. They were to report to the National Guard Armory in Milwaukee where they would be transported to Fort McCoy in west central Wisconsin for several weeks of preparation and training. Beyond that, in typical military fashion, the orders were vague, stating only that their unit would be deployed overseas. Leadership confirmed that their destination was, ultimately, Iraq but supplied no other specifics.

U.S. troops had been massing in Kuwait for several months by the time Charity wrote her Christmas letter. The invasion of Iraq was imminent, but Rachel and Michelle's orders came several weeks before the bombs began to fall on March 20, 2003. It would take weeks to pack-up the 32nd MPs, and it would be at least two months before they actually set foot in Iraq. We prayed that the political pundits were correct, that the Americans would be greeted as liberators by a grateful Iraq and that the war would be essentially over by the time the 32nd MPs arrived.

There were cars to sell, leases to break, and classes to drop. Rachel and Michelle had two weeks to get their affairs in order and report for duty. They were being pulled in a hundred different directions by friends and family who wanted to make sure they could spend time with them before they left. Lori came to the rescue by having an open house, inviting any and all who wanted to say goodbye to our girls. We received neighbors, high school friends and teachers, coworkers and, of course, aunts, uncles, and cousins.

We had been through goodbyes before, but this was different. Behind every farewell, behind every hug, there was the understanding that these young women were going off to war; there were unspoken fears: *"I don't know what I'd do if you got hurt,"* or *"How would I go on if you didn't come home?"* The somber undertone wove itself into the revelry of the party.

Lori had listed a starting time on the invitation but no ending time. Like a campfire, we enjoyed the evening until the very last ember had gone out. For the immediate family, this would be the first of many sendoffs but we need them all. It would take several of these rehearsals to prepare us for the final goodbye, for that day in April when we would drop them at their barracks and hug them for the last time before they crossed the ocean.

On the morning of March 19, 2003, the public gathered at the Richard Street Armory in Milwaukee for the sendoff of the Wisconsin National Guard's 32nd MP Company. It was just one day before the shooting war began in Iraq. The 1920s-era Armory was jammed with reporters, politicians, and family members doing their best to keep a stiff upper lip. We knew from our boot-camp graduation experience that we needed to arrive early if we wanted a seat. We sat, waiting for the ceremony to begin, as the chairs on the platform were arranged and rearranged to accommodate local, county, state, and federal politicians. The community had gathered to give the Wisconsin National Guard's 32nd MP Company a proper sendoff, but first the dignitaries had to be seated in the proper order, and the roster seemed to be changing by the minute. The governor, the mayor, military officials, and members of congress all needed to be accommodated. Regardless of their position on the invasion of Iraq, each of these officials would stand before the cameras and make sure the community knew they supported our troops.

As we waited for our soldiers to arrive, Lori recognized someone in the crowd. This was never a surprise. Lori seemed to know half the people in the greater Milwaukee area. Countless times, I had witnessed people walking up to her and greeting her warmly with Lori responding in kind. Later, when I would ask, "Who was that?" Lori would often reply, "I have no idea." Most recognized her from her job as a fitness instructor. Lori taught classes at various clubs nearly every day of the week, and it would be difficult to tell you what she enjoyed more, teaching classes or chatting up the people who attended them.

The woman Lori recognized was Yami. Lori, Rachel, Charity, and Michelle had met Yami at a poetry reading several weeks earlier. Coincidentally, Yami was a reporter for Milwaukee's CBS affiliate. Lori explained that Rachel and Michelle were in the National Guard and that we were here to see them off, and she went on to explain that Charity was also a Guard member, serving with the Company B 118th Medical Battalion based in Waukesha.

Yami doubled as a journalist for Milwaukee's Spanish-language channel and was very active in the community. Both roles gave her a great deal of contact with politicians, which may explain her boldness when she decided that the governor should know about the family with three daughters serving in the National Guard, two of them deploying with the 32nd MPs. After the ceremony, she buttonholed Governor Jim Doyle's aide and suggested that it would be very appropriate for the governor to greet us personally.

As we spoke to the governor, cameras began to roll and reporters picked up the story of the family with three daughters in the National Guard. The fact that Michelle and Charity were twins seemed to add to the fascination. That evening we would watch ourselves on the news, shaking hands with the governor and answering questions about our soldier-daughters. In the months to come, we would often give follow-up interviews, updating the southeast-Wisconsin-viewing audience on our daughters. A year later, a worldwide audience would see the Witmer family on camera.

Fort McCoy is about three hours northwest of Milwaukee near Sparta, Wisconsin, and it was the 32nd MP's first stop on their journey to Iraq. There would be several weeks of intense training and briefings. The leadership granted one final leave before our soldiers shipped out, but they were restricted to a distance of no more than seventy-five miles from Fort McCoy. New Berlin is 170 miles from Fort McCoy, and even if distance wasn't an issue, Rachel and Michelle, like the other soldiers, had either sold their vehicles or left them behind. So Charity, Tim, Mark, Lori, and I made plans to pick them up and whisk them away for one last weekend together. We drove through the base, following the map we were given at the guard house, and ended up in an area that looked like it was straight out of a World War II movie. There were old, gray, two-story, boxy buildings that served as barracks. Inside there was one long room with rows of neatly made beds, heads to the wall and foot lockers on the aisle.

The soldiers could not start their leave until they attended a briefing that would restate what everyone already knew—that they had to be back by 4:00 p.m. Sunday and that they could not travel more than seventy-five miles from the base. Military families get used to waiting, but we were anxious to start our weekend, and the redundant briefing was especially trying, completely expected but trying all the same.

We rented a suite at a hotel in the Wisconsin Dells, a resort area about forty miles from the base. We had planned to spend some time rattling around the tourist traps, but it was early in the season and the weather was cold and rainy. Instead, we settled in the hotel room, playing cards for hours, talking, reading, and napping. Occasionally we would venture out to the indoor water park, but we spent most the time just being with each other, soaking in our time together, not knowing how long this weekend together would need to last us.

Rachel, Michelle, and Charity all shared one king-size bed. For this one night, I could imagine they were our little girls again. For one night I could believe that they were all safely tucked in bed, that the world was a simple place where I could stand watch over them.

The weather broke on Sunday, and we wandered up and down the main street of the Wisconsin Dells, taking in the arcades and souvenir shops, enjoying the sunny but chilly day; we had no agenda except to be together. Nothing puts time in perspective like sending a soldier off to war; we were aware of every minute that slipped by. In any other context, the day might have seemed boring, but we wanted to stretch every second. We wanted to draw out the conversations, and if there were no words, we just wanted to sit with each other.

When we could delay no longer, we set out for Fort McCoy for the goodbye that would have to last for a year or more, seeing our soldiers off on a mission that would involve danger on a level I had only seen in movies. I wasn't feeling particularly patriotic that day. I joked about passing the exit to Fort McCoy and driving north to Canada, and if my girls had given me any indication that they didn't want to go back to the base, I think I would have done it. We pulled up to the ancient barracks, and as they stepped out of the car, my little girls disappeared, replaced by proud, competent, young women who were ready for their mission. We said goodbye and left them as they were preparing for formation. I don't remember talking much on the way home.

Chapter 6 – Like Sands through the Hour Glass

Michelle and Rachel arrived in Kuwait with the 32nd MPs, shortly after President George W. Bush made what came to be known as his "mission accomplished" speech on the deck of USS Abraham Lincoln on May 1, 2003. In my mind, that meant the shooting war would be over by the time Michelle and Rachel entered Iraq and that, with any luck, they would be assigned to some boring security detail. I imagined them sitting in a guard shack at the entrance to a supply depot, collecting signatures and paperwork as trucks came and went. What I didn't know was the standing joke among the reservist is that "MP" stood for "multi-purpose" and that Rachel and Michelle would be in the middle of a war without frontlines.

Everyone wanted the latest information about Rachel and Michelle; aunts and uncles, high school friends, neighbors, and even local reporters, and it seemed that no matter how hard we tried, we always missed someone. About a month after my daughters were deployed, I created the "Witmer Family Website." I put up the website in part, to meet the ongoing request for updates, but there was another reason; in a time before social-networking websites made creating websites easy, it gave me something useful to do and a way to channel my energy. I tinkered with software and worked with my Internet provider to create the site. I posted any pictures and e-mails Rachel and Michelle sent us, and I summarized any phone calls we received. Later, when they had Internet access, Rachel and Michelle could post messages directly to the website and know that they could reach the entire extended family in one shot.

Michelle posted her first message on the site describing the base in Kuwait: "So here I am yesterday, and the temperature got up to 127 degrees. It is hot and sandy and did I mention hot. I saw a herd of camels yesterday, the highlight of my day I might add." Her combination of sarcasm and wit always brought a smile to my face. She would get in character and lecture like an old schoolteacher, with a staccato delivery, and I could hear that tone in these words she wrote:

A brief summary of my living conditions: We have two platoons per tent. The tents are about the size of an Olympic-size pool, just big open space. We do not have cots; we sleep on the ground on our sleeping bags. As you can imagine, it's not air conditioned and, yes, we do still have to wear our full DCU's (Desert Camo Uniforms.) There are about 70 people per tent. We actually do get 10-minute showers if we're lucky enough, after we wait in line and the water doesn't run out. ... I feel like I'm going to die of heat, but they have us drinking loads and loads of water. There are constantly Blackhawks and other helicopters flying overhead. They have "Discovery Channel" snakes. My time's up.

Michelle was part clown. She and her brothers and sisters had grown up understanding the value of humor, and they found ways to make each other laugh on a daily basis; it was almost a competition. When you're thousands of miles from home, taking enemy fire on a regular basis, making people laugh can be a gift, a gift Michelle used to benefit those around her. In one e-mail she told me this:

I walked into a pole today because I was not looking where I was going. It was like something out of a cartoon. Everyone laughed, because it was very funny. I felt stupid but I took a bow and laughed right along. I told them I did it on purpose for comic relief.

It wasn't that Michelle was clumsy, she was klutzy. The difference is that clumsiness is something you're born with. Klutziness is what happens when your mind is always a couple of steps ahead of your body. Michelle was on the eighth grade cheerleading squad, ran cross-country, played soccer and softball, and was a good dancer; she knew how to move. The fact that she sometimes walked into poles would seem incongruous unless you understood that she was a deep thinker and that poles sometimes jump out in front of you when you are deep in thought.

Michelle earned the reputation for being klutzy over the course of her deployment. One of her buddies told this story about her:

We're headed out, one day, so we jump into the Humvee. Michelle's driving and I'm riding shotgun. I look over and I see Michelle slumped over the steering wheel, and I watch as she loses consciousness. A million thoughts are going through my mind and I yell out, "GAS! GAS! GAS!" as I scramble to put on my mask. I see a flurry of activity as everyone around me pulls on their masks.

Michelle's eyes begin to twitch open and the first thing she sees is me looking back at her with my gasmask on and she starts scrambling to put on her mask. I yell, "Witmer! Are you okay!" but I have my mask on and she can't make out what I'm saying.

Michelle looks back, panic in her eyes and says, "What the hell is going on!"

"You passed out!"

Michelle just stares.

"You passed out," I say again, louder and slower so she can hear me through my mask.

Michelle looks away and says nothing for a moment and then fesses up: "I hit my shin on the steering column. It hurt so bad I must have passed out."

For days after that, 2nd Platoon kept up the razzing, slumping to the ground in mock fainting spells whenever Michelle walked by, staying down just long enough to make sure she saw them and then springing back up to laugh themselves silly.

Rachel found her own way to keep life interesting during the long, slow days in Kuwait. By June, she was growing tired of waiting around and she wrote, "I don't know how much longer we will be at this camp before we get a mission, but all of the sudden I just want to leave here and get it over with. I can't even pretend that there is an end in sight until we are on whatever mission they give us." She continued with this story:

My friend, Beth and I were really bored last week and we heard around camp that people had brought swim suits to go sunbathing. We asked our Sergeant about it and he said *absolutely not!* He didn't want us sunburned or seen by anyone (both valid concerns in hindsight, which is always 20/20.) Beth got angry and told me she felt like he was treating us like children. After much coaxing (and it took a *lot*), she got me to sneak off with her later that afternoon.

The company next to us has about 30 flatbed trucks that are about six feet off the ground. If you lay down inside of them, you're not visible except from above. So our brilliant idea was to lay out in the back of one of these trucks. It would have been a flawlessly executed plan, only we were followed! We stripped down to our bras and a head popped over the side of the truck. It was our company Doc; needless to say our Sergeant was pretty upset when he found out.

Right now I am in a restricted status and I have rules and limitations on where and when I can go places. Not to mention with whom.

… So, on the whole, I'm going *insane.* Thank goodness for Shelly, she is my port in the storm and the only thing keeping me sane. We lean on each other a lot here, and I am more thankful for her every day.

I was glad Rachel and Michelle had each other to lean on. They had always been close, looking out for each other; Michelle, in fact, sometimes, took it to the extreme. Shortly before she left for boot camp, Rachel dated a young man named Luke. Michelle didn't like Luke, and she made no attempt to conceal that fact. Luke was handsome but a little too cavalier for Michelle's taste. Michelle contended that Rachel was only dating him because she was bored.

At the time, we lived in a huge, old house with a mother-in-law apartment on the second floor. The apartment had its own entrance, serviced by some rickety wooden stairs. We used the apartment's living room as the family's TV room, and the apartment's only bedroom belong to Rachel. As if to confirm the family's opinion of his character, Luke made a habit of avoiding the front door and slinking up the back stairs. One fateful December day Luke happened to slip in while Michelle was watching TV, and she took it upon herself to become the family spokesperson. She cornered Luke, and getting right up in his face, she let loose, "So you're coming in the back door again?! Why are you sneaking around!? Is it because you know *none of us like you*! Do you know what we call you? We call you 'Luke the

Puke!' You're not good enough for Rachel and you never will be, so do us all a favor and *get lost!"*

Rachel intervened before Michelle dismembered Luke, ushering him down the back steps. I don't know if Michelle's tirade had anything to do with it, but a few weeks later Rachel stopped seeing Luke.

On Father's Day I received an e-mail from Michelle that haunted me in the weeks to come. She explained that the 32nd would be leaving the relative safety of Camp Virginia and driving several hundred miles north to Baghdad.

> We had a briefing telling us to prepare ourselves as best as possible for what lies ahead. Things like children running out in front of the vehicles to try and get them to stop; we have to prepare ourselves to hit people, because stopping is not an option. I guess every convoy that's gone up north so far has taken fire or been ambushed. The question of whether we will or not is not even really a question, more like a guess as to when. These things, as you can imagine, are a lot to take in.

I worried not only about my daughters' physical safety, I worried about the emotional scars the war might leave on them. Thinking about Michelle, faced with a choice between endangering her convoy or running down a child, made my blood run cold. I wondered who my daughters would be when they returned, whether they would still be able to smile and laugh.

An e-mail from Rachel followed shortly after Michelle's: "We will be moving out of here soon, and when we do, I will probably not be able to contact you guys for a good 30-45 days." My daughters were heading into a war zone, and it would be weeks before we received news from them. It would be the longest weeks of our lives.

> You will probably get a letter from me before you hear from me by phone or e-mail. I will be checking this e-mail account through the week but I can't promise anything after that. I am supposed to tell you guys not to contact the Red Cross or Family Support if you hear something on the news about the death or injury of an American soldier in our area. If it concerns anyone from our company, they will contact you. So basically no news is good news.

You don't have to worry though! Shelly and I are quite capable of taking care of ourselves! Most of the casualties over here so far have literally been the result of stupidity on the part of the soldier. Shelly and I have our heads in the game and we are looking forward to starting our mission.

Rachel's claim that there was nothing to worry about seemed a little too enthusiastic. Her own worry seemed to seep through the assurances. "If we stop responding to your e-mails for a while, *don't stop writing us!* We will get to computers at least once a month if they don't provide them in our immediate living area. I will be able to check my email one more time before I leave, but I probably won't have time to write, just read."

And after that e-mail, all communication stopped. Even though they said it would be a month before we heard anything, we still checked for e-mails, we still hoped for a letter in the mailbox. But it was as they had told us. It would be weeks before we heard from them again, weeks before we received a letter written from the capital of a country at war.

Chapter 7 - Strangers in a Strange Land

Rachel was twenty-three when the Wisconsin National Guard convoyed from Kuwait to Baghdad; Michelle was just nineteen. At the time, there were about 150,000 U.S. troops deployed in Iraq, far less than the 450,000 troops some experts said were necessary to maintain control of the country. Baghdad's population is nearly eight million people, and the 32nd's mission was to restore police protection through a combination of patrolling the streets and training a reconstituted Iraq police force.

When they arrived, living conditions were primitive—no running water which meant no toilets or showers. They dug latrines, lived on dehydrated food packets called "MREs" (Meals Ready to Eat) and had no access to the Internet. As I waited for an update, I thought about families of soldiers in generations past whose only link to their loved one was the postal system. The days passed like weeks as we waited for word from Baghdad. The third week of July, three weeks after their convoy left Kuwait, the postman dropped a letter in our mailbox. Michelle's block print graced the front of the envelope and the words "free mail" appeared in the upper-right corner. The sheets of paper inside the envelope were ragged on the left where they had been torn from a standard issue college-ruled notebook.

She was okay. At least she was okay as of July 4th, the day she had penned the letter. Before I read the first word, I was filled with the joy and relief that only this knowledge could bring me.

> … Well, I've been in Baghdad for close to a week now
> and it's like nothing I could have ever imagined! We are
> staying at what was once a beautiful country-club home
> that belonged to one of Saddam's close advisors. He was
> a known terrorist and "The King of Spades" in the deck of
> cards with all Saddam's advisors and most wanted.

Michelle, along with all the soldiers serving in the theater, had been given a deck of playing cards that featured pictures of Iraq's "most wanted," members of Saddam Hussein's regime. When these men were captured, the news reports would make mention of their ranking in the deck of cards. The face cards were reserved for the highest ranking members of Saddam's government.

At one time this place must have been spectacularly beautiful but it was bombed pretty badly and now all that's left is crumbling buildings and remnants of marble floors and staircases, gold door knobs and light fixtures and half-burned Persian rugs. It truly must have been grand. The grounds are beautiful with palm trees and flowers and all the gardens and grass are overgrown but at one time I'm sure they were perfectly manicured and the gardens—well, I can only imagine. It's really more like a palace.

Ever the aspiring journalist, she wrote the letter as if she were a war correspondent filing a report. I marveled at her talent. Her handwriting stood in stark contrast to her ability to turn a phrase. Michelle had grown up in the computer age so it was rare that she had to write anything by hand. Her block print was rough and hurried—as if her hand had struggled to keep up with the thoughts she recorded.

It's really heartbreaking to see the poverty right outside the gates where we live and think about how Saddam and his crew were living. The children literally swarm you. Smiling little toddlers wave and cry after us saying, "misses, misses—please water, please food." These children usually wander around in filthy clothes and no shoes. Some of them can't be more than four-years old. It breaks my heart not to be able to give them anything.

The police station I work at is in the worst part of Baghdad. The only thing I can compare it to is maybe the worst part of New York's or Chicago's ghettos except with no justice system. We are the police and right now the city is in chaos and it's going to take a long, long time to make even a small dent. There are no working stoplights or traffic signs. The traffic is unreal. People drive like maniacs.

Yesterday morning there was a drive-by in front of our station and two Iraqis were killed, shot in the head in their car. The station is sort of like the Mexican police stations in movies, a filthy little hole in the wall run by crooked cops who are poor and don't have much to lose. There are no doors except for the one that locks in the prisoners. Two of the people in our holding cell are murderers. Then there are a bunch of thieves and looters and a few minors who we hold overnight and then release.

I work the night shift, 7 p.m. to 7a.m. It's very frightening being in the worst ghetto you can ever imagine, at night, in the dark, and not only do we have to worry about the common criminal gang activity but also the pockets of resistance who still support Saddam. They frequently shoot at our building and are very much a threat. I hear gunfire all the time, it's so unnerving! Last night Rachel's station, which is a *lot* nicer than mine, got attacked. No one was hurt but it was scary and they returned fire.

Any hopes I had that Michelle and Rachel would be sitting in a guard shack at some equipment storage depot, far away from danger, evaporated as I read the letter. It would take several more months and many more e-mails, letters and phone calls before I would fully grasp the danger my daughter's faced, day in and day out.

I sat and talked to the Arabic interpreters for a long time last night. There are two and they both are fluent in English. One of them is also fluent in Russian and the other also speaks Chinese, it's amazing. They are teaching me three words a day in Arabic. Wow, is it difficult!

One of them used to work at an Iraqi television studio, before the war, as a sound tech. But he was thrown into prison after there was an audio problem with one of Saddam's speeches. Saddam's men beat him and smashed his hands. They are pretty much healed but his nails will be black forever. He was thrown in prison for two months, and by prison I mean a tiny cell underground with no windows and about 25 other men. He said that he was on the verge of death, his fifth day without food or water. He said he would feel for puddles on the bottom of the cell floor (he couldn't see because it was pitch black underground) and try to lick up anything he could find. Two men had already died from lack of food and water. Then the Marines came and broke down the door and gave everyone water.

"They asked me if I could walk home, I told them yes."

He said his family was so happy to see him alive. He said
he still has dreams about it. This was an educated college
grad, fluent in many languages, who made a mistake on
the sound board. Saddam was evil. It's overwhelming to
talk, first hand, to these Iraqis and glimpse the insanity.

In the months and years that would follow, many would question
the U.S. invasion of Iraq. The story of this interpreter stayed with me
as did Michelle's pronouncement that "Saddam was evil." Her words,
written from the heart of Baghdad, carried more weight than a hundred
political commentaries. She finished with these words: "Please pray for
me, this is no cake walk. I love you all so much. I'll try to write again
soon."

This letter, this first letter from Baghdad, was circulated first to
Charity, then Tim, then Mark, and then to the extended family via the
family website. Lori kept the original in her purse until it was dog-
eared and wearing thin at the creases. She read it so many times she
didn't have to look at it when she recited Michelle's words to anyone
she could get to listen. She clung to it like a treasure.

Lori tells the story of a "girls' night" she had with Rachel,
Michelle and Charity when they were in high school. They decided to
watch the tear-jerker *Steel Magnolias*, and at the end of the movie,
Lori, Rachel and Michelle were sobbing while Charity sat on the couch
with her arms folded. "It's just a *movie!*" she admonished.

I've always marveled how different my children are, how they
emerged from the womb with discernable personalities. Michelle was
sensitive to a fault; Charity, although empathetic, was equal parts
pragmatic. Rachel was the artist, talented and capable of great
accomplishments when the spirit moved her, but uninterested in the
mundane tasks of life, like balancing her checkbook or checking the oil
in her car. Michelle was a worrier, and she wrote more often because
she worried that *we* were worrying. And it was right in character for
Rachel to take much longer to write us.

We received Rachel's first e-mail about three weeks after she left
Kuwait. "I work so much that I don't have time to think about anything
but work," she wrote. The statement was oddly comforting to me. I
was glad she could lose herself in her work. It seemed to be the best
way to push through the deployment. She wrote less frequently than
Michelle, but when the spirit moved her, it was compelling reading.

She explained that their unit had been quartered in what had likely been servants' housing on a compound that used to contain one of Saddam's palaces, "before we bombed the heck out of it." She went on to describe the glory of working showers, the promise of air conditioning and a typical day in Baghdad. "Right now I am working the night shift at one of the Baghdad Police stations. It's a 12-hour shift from 7 p.m. to 7 a.m. but keeping busy makes the time go by pretty fast, though."

I could see Rachel, in my mind's eye, focused and absorbed in her work. I worried less about her not only because she was four years older than Michelle but because she seemed better able to keep the war at an emotional distance.

> It's been really hard to sleep during the day in the heat, but my body is adjusting. I am up again by 4:00 pm to do PT (Physical Training) and prep for my shift. That makes about six hours of sleep a day; needless to say I am tired! I get a day off every eight days, and that thought is about the only thing that keeps me going. On the upside, the pool inside of our compound was not badly damaged in the bombing.

I suspected that both Rachel and Michelle filtered what they shared with me. I was always trying to read between the lines—trying to understand how they were *really* feeling. As the months went on, my suspicions were confirmed. I was talking to Charity when there was an awkward pause in the conversation. Charity realized that she had mentioned an event that Michelle had chosen not to share with me.

"What murder scene?" I quizzed.

"Oh, it wasn't that big of a deal," Charity backpedaled. "I'm sure she'll tell you about it, but you should hear it from her."

But Michelle never told me about it, which meant it must have been really hard for her and, as always, she didn't want to worry me. I pieced the story together a little at a time, coaxing details out of those Michelle had confided. To put the event in context, it's helpful to understand how the MPs operated. The theory was that if the MPs worked side-by-side with the Iraqi police (IPs), eventually the IPs would adopt the American style of police work. Under Saddam's rule, the typical IP spent his day in the police station. If people in the neighborhood needed help, they came to the station; patrolling neighborhoods was not how the IPs operated. Now the MPs would patrol the neighborhoods and the IPs would reluctantly follow along.

On this particular day, a call came in about a homicide and Michelle's team responded, weaving through the littered streets in their Humvees until they found the address. As they approached the house they could hear mournful wailing and they entered to find a middle-aged man and his inconsolable wife. The interpreter worked to piece together the story for the team. The man explained that his daughter was rebellious and disrespectful; that she had continued to defy him. He said he could not allow her to continue to shame the family.

In the adjoining room, Michelle saw what could only have been his daughter. She was a teenager, lovely dark hair and complexion, dressed in traditional clothing. She was hanging next to a table, a wire around her neck, her lovely brown eyes staring out from half-closed lids.

Michelle helped as the soldiers, with as much dignity as possible, took the body down.

She worked the scene as she had been trained to do, taking statements, snapping pictures, and completing reports. She had been through difficult situations before, but this time she had held death in her arms, and saw, firsthand, the destruction it left in its wake. I knew my daughter, I knew the mark this would leave on her soul, and I continued to wonder what she would be like when she returned to me.

Rachel would see her share of the ugliness of war. On those rare occasions when she found time to write a long letter home, she would describe her world: "It is an interesting situation, some of the IP's used to work for the police during Saddam's reign and now claim that 'they love Americans', so we can literally trust no one. I carry two loaded weapons at all times inside the PD, and sit on the toilet with a loaded pistol at the ready." She continued:

> There are virtually no set laws right now. We could bring in three people who all committed the exact same crime, and depending on the mood of the IPs, each of them would be dealt with differently. They don't understand the concept of 'use of force,' and will go as far as to shoot a person in the head for stealing a car. I showed up for work, a few days ago, and there was a pickup truck parked

in front of the police station with a dead man's body lying in the back. The IPs shot him in the head for stealing. His face was barely recognizable as a face. I had never seen a corpse before.

There was a crowd gathered just silent and staring. One woman was screaming and wailing, in mourning. It was the most awful sound I think I have ever heard. I think the man had been her husband. She was tearing out huge clumps of her hair and ripping her clothes as she screamed and cried. It was horrible to watch. She started beating herself in the face and chest until she was bruised and bloodied by her own hands. Finally, some of the bystanders held her down and took her away.

I wondered how often she would see this scene in her dreams. Would it wake her up with a start in the middle of the night? Would she encounter a place, a smell, or a sound that would bring it all rushing back at the most unexpected moments? I remember feeling so powerless; I was learning that no one goes to war and returns unscathed.

It was one of the longest letters Rachel sent home, and I felt like she *needed* to write it, like she would have rather had a long talk, but short of that she needed to frame these thoughts.

The language barrier is difficult, but not impossible with the help of translators. All of our translators are men between the ages of 20 and 30 who want to find sponsors and go to America. I have been proposed to by all three, and upon rejection, they moved on to the other three women in our squad. Some of the IPs have proposed as well, I have even been asked to be a 2nd wife! Needless to say the Iraqi men *love* American women, but they don't respect us at all.

In Iraq, women are taught to be submissive. If a man looks them in the eyes, they are taught to look away. Female soldiers are told to stare back until they look away in order to show that we are not passive. I have literally been in two to three minute staring contests with defiant men who finally give up. … I'm sorry if this seems choppy, but all of this is really hard for me to write about. If I write about what I am doing here it means I have to think about what I am doing here, and my job is really hard to process and deal with right now.

I didn't need to read between the lines this time and now I realized that her honesty was both a blessing and a curse. If she had continued to avoid writing about the hard things she faced, I could have at least pretended that it wasn't as bad as I thought. Now I knew what she was going through; I knew she would be coming home changed.

We lived for those rare phone calls from Iraq. We got the first call from Michelle several weeks after they arrived in Baghdad. The phone rang at about three o'clock in the morning and after a brief delay we heard Michelle's voice say "hello." We erupted with a mix of ecstatic greetings and a barrage of questions while Michelle did the best she could to answer them all. The connection was awful. She was calling on a satellite phone; there were delays and static, and sometimes the connection would cut out to white noise or a screeching sound. The calls rarely ended with "goodbye." After talking around the noise the call would drop, usually in mid-sentence. We would hang on the phone to see if her voice might reemerge from the noise and after we waited much longer than it was logical to do, we would hang up, feeling both elated and despondent at the same time. Elated, because we got to hear her voice, despondent, because we had only begun to have a conversation and then it was over.

We went to great lengths to make sure we would never miss a call. I programmed our home phone to hunt through a list of cell phones if no one answered at the house. I had my cell phone with me constantly and ran out of a church service more than once to take a call that had been forwarded from home. As the months went by, Rachel and Michelle had access to land lines and the calls got better and longer. Occasionally we could have a real conversation and it was on one of these calls that Michelle told Lori this story:

Michelle explained that the IPs had a lunchtime ritual. They sat in a circle, ate their meal, and then smoked the hookah. They filled the bowl of a tall, bottle-shaped pipe with flavored tobacco and drew in the smoke through a small hose with a mouthpiece attached. The water in the hookah cooled the smoke, making it easy to inhale, and as they smoked, the fragrance of fruit and tobacco would fill the room. Smoke-filled rooms were the norm in Iraq. Most of the IPs smoked like chimneys. Michelle was not a smoker, but when the IPs invited her to smoke with them after lunch, Michelle realized the importance of the invitation. The IPs were inviting a female soldier to sit with them; she was literally being accepted into their circle.

From that time on she had a weakness for flavored tobacco and she enjoyed an occasional smoke; it steadied the nerves, she said, and something about being in a war zone eclipses the fear of the long-term consequences.

As a child, Michelle would pass out at the sight of blood. She fainted dead away when she got vaccinations, which made it all the more amazing when I received an e-mail explaining that she often acted as the first responder to a whole range of injuries.

In our station we joke that we should be a medical unit. because almost every night we end up treating some person the IPs bring in bleeding. So far I've dealt with massive trauma to the head (a street gang beat this guy's head in with a crowbar), a bunch of people with bullet wounds in various places (arms, legs, chest), stab wounds also in various places, and broken bones. I always think about Aunt Teresa because she works in the ER and we do so much emergency medical care.

… Last night these two young Iraqis pulled an old man out of his car and beat him almost to the point of death and stole his car. They were high on some type of drugs. The Iraqi police came on the scene and beat the two criminals and then brought them back to the station. They showed up with the two young guys bleeding from the head very badly. When we questioned the IPs about how they were hurt, they explained that's the way they treat criminals. They both needed to go to a hospital, but the medical system in Baghdad is terrible. We sent one prisoner to the hospital to be treated for a bullet wound and they brought him back a half-hour later with a little bit of gauze over the wound.

Last night when I was treating one of the carjackers; it was the first time it got to me a little bit. Usually I go through the motions and the procedures and everything's fine. There was an unusually large amount of blood, and,

43

for the first time since I've been here, I almost vomited. I held it together and didn't let on to anyone that I was almost about to throw up. I guess you just can't think too much about what's going on. Well, I have to get going but I love you all so much. Please continue to pray for me. I wish I had some idea of when I was coming home.

But Michelle held back one medical story, a story I would only hear about years after her deployment. One evening, four critically injured Iraqis showed up at the door of the police station, victims of domestic violence. An angry uncle was threatening to detonate a grenade when it accidentally went off in his hand. The explosion removed his arm and sent shrapnel into a pregnant mother and her two small girls. Michelle and her team rendered first aid, but the brass decided it was too dangerous to take the family to the hospital. A vehicle arrived to transport the man who had lost his arm, but the mother and daughters would have to wait until the IPs arranged for another ambulance.

Michelle sat with one of the little girls on her lap, comforting the girl as she struggled for breath, fighting the shrapnel wound in her chest. She held her for over an hour, rocking her, stroking her hair, before the IPs arrived to transport her to the hospital, but an hour later Michelle would learn that the little girl didn't make it.

As females, Rachel and Michelle dealt not only with the hardships of war but with all the baggage that comes with being a woman in the military. Michelle's wrote:

It's a constant battle for respect being a woman over here, I've learned to keep the same expression on my face and not smile too much. I am the only female in my squad so I work with virtually all men. When I go back to base camp all I want to do is find my friend Jackson (Shizuko), and talk to her about things women talk about (Mom, you know what I mean.)

I love getting mail and appreciate it so very much. If you only knew how it feels to come "home" to the compound and see a piece of mail on your cot after a long night at the station. Sometimes it makes me cry. It's just a little reminder that someone back home is thinking about me and supports me through all this. I love you all so much.

Michelle and Rachel were not complainers by nature. When we got e-mails, like this one, we knew they need to vent, that they needed to write down the struggles they were going through. My hope was that letters, like this were cathartic, that hitting the send button on the computer gave them the assurance that people who loved and cared about them would be reading their words empathizing with them and praying for them.

There were plenty of e-mails with lighter tones. In late August, Rachel wrote, "I had a day off yesterday and got to spend some time by the pool. It was *heaven!* Aside from the bombed out buildings all around me, I almost forgot where I was." Michelle followed that up with a weather report and some requests. I had written that our next door neighbor, a WWII vet, had been updating us on the summer weather in Baghdad. Michelle responded.

> Mr. Miller would be correct in saying it's 135 in Baghdad, like 120 in the shade. It's one of the hottest summers on record. Lucky us huh! As far as a wish list goes here are a few things I dream about:
> - Crystal light - you can't send enough of the stuff
> - DVD's (mind you this is a wish list I don't expect anything)
> - CD's any new music were so starved for anything new here
> - Magazines -People, Cosmo, Marie Claire, US weekly—I mean anything at all
> - A pair of flip flops size 7 ½
> - Good facial moisturizer
> - Laundry detergent
> - Pictures of all of you!!!!!!
> - Some chocolate (ooh the cravings)
> - Anything that is frivolous like a self-heating face mask or stuff along those lines. I like to feel like a girl again sometimes.
>
> Okay, there it is—no obligation whatsoever.
>
> Love you all.

I never felt like I did enough for my daughters when they were overseas. We sent them care packages, but I always felt like we should be sending more. We wrote to them, but it didn't seem like I wrote often enough. Even though Rachel and Michelle had regular Internet access, I knew they liked getting letters. The problem with trying to write a letter every day or even every other day is that you run out of things to write about. All the back-home news had been covered in e-mails and it was hard to come up with anything interesting to put down on paper. I eventually found a creative solution, one that prompted Rachel to write, "I got one of your 'special' postcards yesterday! The first of nine, I had a hard time explaining to my Platoon Sergeant what it was supposed to be! He thought it was hilarious."

I had written Rachel and Michelle, telling them that I had grown a goatee. I took a snapshot of my "new look," blew it up, and then cut it into post-card-sized pieces. I stamped all nine pieces and mailed one a day for nine days with only a cryptic note on the back, "one-of-nine", "two-of-nine," and so on. It gave Rachel and Michelle both a puzzle to solve and a post card to look forward to.

What Rachel and Michelle didn't know was the reason I grew the goatee. I worried constantly and the worry was taking a physical toll. I started having severe stomach problems and eventually went to the doctor. I laughed out loud when he asked me if I was under any kind of stress. I tried several different medications with little effect, but the one thing that seemed to provide temporary relief was snacking. When my stomach hurt, I ate, and consequently I put on a lot of weight. I grew the goatee to camouflage my double chin.

October brought a very disturbing email from Michelle; in it she described a harrowing episode while out on patrol the night before. She described lights flickering in the distance but she couldn't make out what they were; she only knew the lights shouldn't be there. Eleven hours into her twelve-hour shift, fatigue had begun to sink in, making it that much more difficult to sort out the strange lights lining both sides of the road. The patrol rolled in to investigate, moving slowly, when they caught sight of a man frantically waving his arms, beckoning the soldiers to come to him. They rolled through the lights and approached the agitated man.

The interpreter had to settle the man down before he could to make sense of what he was saying, but then he understood. The lights were a trap and they had done exactly what they were supposed to do: luring the patrol in to investigate. An IED had been buried in the road, waiting to do its killing.

As the morning wore on, they found out that a faulty remote detonator had save their lives. At the moment they rolled through the trap, an insurgent, stationed within watching distance, had pressed the button on a remote control. But nothing happened. No detonation. No explosion. Maybe the device was out of range, maybe the batteries in the remote were weak, or maybe the bomb was wired incorrectly.

It wasn't until the unit returned to camp that Michelle began to understand the magnitude of what she had just been through. A malfunction had saved her life. She should have been killed. "As I thought about how close I came to dying, everything around me changed; the air smelled sweeter, that the sky looked bluer, and as I gazed up, I saw a flock of doves take flight. They reminded me of the passage in the Bible when the Spirit of God descended like a dove. God seemed so close and I was so thankful to be alive."

Rachel wrote: "We've been hearing buzzing from people who know what they are talking about, and as of right now, we might be home just in time for Christmas! We hear rumors all of the time, but this came out of the Battalion SGT Major's own mouth, and he doesn't spread empty rumors. Here's hoping!"

The dream of being home for Christmas was short-lived. Only a few weeks later, the families of the 32nd MPs would receive a letter explaining that their soldier's tour of duty had been extended indefinitely. The world "indefinitely" seemed so cavalier. How could anyone with even the slightest understanding of what it's like to wait for a soldier use the word "indefinitely?" It was so cold, so callous. At a meeting called by the $32^{nd's}$ family support group, I listened to one heart wrenching story after another: a mother of small children was trying to keep her husband's business afloat; a soldier's wife was trying to make ends meet on a military salary that was a fraction her spouse's civilian income. "Disappointment" did not begin to describe the mood.

I got angry. At the risk of being branded a subversive, I fired off a letter to the White House, addressed to President Bush: "Imagine how you would feel if your daughters were patrolling the streets of Baghdad; imagine worrying about them every day, and then imagine what it would be like to have no idea when they were coming home." I included a picture of Rachel and Michelle. There was no response from the White House, and I imagined the letter going into some FBI file and my name being added to a database of "undesirables."

I had raised my daughters to be independent. To do otherwise would have dishonored my mother's memory. Like many women of her generation, my mother took a subservient role. My father was the breadwinner and therefore the head of the household. My mother waited on him hand and foot, cleaning, cooking, and even laying out his clothes. One day when I was about ten, my mother called me over to the ironing board where she was toiling over a pile of shirts. She began teaching me how properly iron a shirt, and when she was done, she said, "You're going to learn to take care of yourself, and you're never going to treat a woman this way."

It was her influence that shaped the way I raised my children. My girls always believed that there were no limits, that they could do any job they put their mind to; but they would find that much of the world wasn't ready for that idea. Rachel wrote us in mid-October. The email started with a lighter tone before shifting to a venting session about a woman in "This Man's Army":

It rained today!! For the first time in eight months, I woke up to a sky full of clouds (there hasn't been a *single* cloud for the last 6 months!) It got darker and darker while I was running, and by 6:00 a.m. the sky *exploded*!! It's still raining four hours later and, if I close my eyes and stand outside, it almost feels like home. The smell is *amazing*. I forgot how great rain smells! Shelly is sitting on the computer next to me typing a letter. We just saw the picture of Charity and all of the orange leaves on the trees and got really homesick. I can't wait to see everyone.

There is a lot of talk going around as to when we are leaving. Most of our officers think that Bush put this "open-ended deployment" thing into place just so that he can lift it and play the hero right before election time. I am really, *really* hoping that's the case! They think we might be home by late January. *Here's hoping.*

Dad, things here are really wearing me down. I have been fighting with everything in me to keep a positive attitude—especially for Shelly's sake, but I am just getting *so* tired. Being a woman on this deployment means that I've had the cards stacked against me from day one. ... No matter what anyone says or tries to make me believe, a good two-thirds of the men in the military believe that women shouldn't be here. ... My PT score is higher than all but two of the men in my platoon (that's by the *men's* scoring standards, too) and yet every day people make degrading comments and treat me like I just don't measure up. Even my direct chain of command treats me as if I am a lesser person!

Dad, I don't want to *be* a man, but I can't stand being treated like a lesser person just because I am a woman. I have been overlooked and ignored, ripped on, stepped on, blamed for problems that I have had *nothing* to do with just because I was the only woman in the situation. My team leader talks about women like they are lower than dirt, on a daily basis, in front of me. As if that weren't bad enough, I work with all Iraqi men that have been *raised not to respect women*!

I ride in the turret of the Humvee, making me the most visible person on our team. I am the one that all of the Iraqis see when we patrol the streets. ... Literally one in every five men (and the streets are packed) either yells something lewd or makes some lewd gesture. Most of them make a display of grabbing their crotch, and thrusting it at me while they obnoxiously lick their lips and moan. Some of them even go so far as to unzip their pants. They yell things like "f--k me baby," or "freaky, freaky," you get the idea. ... I try to look more masculine by wearing dark glasses, but my hair isn't long enough to pull into a ponytail, so it sticks out of the bottom of my helmet, making it obvious that I am a woman. I am not *allowed* to wear a bandana to cover it up! That is, by far, the most pointless rule that we've had so far!

... I got a partial explanation from one of our translators. He told me that the general belief among the Iraqi public is that the women in the U.S. Army aren't soldiers, but whores for the men so that they don't get antsy while we are here. Talk about degrading! Needless to say, I am running out of patience. ...

The sisterhood went beyond blood. Besides watching out for each other, both Rachel and Michelle developed strong bonds with their other sisters-in-arms, and they watched out for each other. There's a picture of Michelle dancing with her friend Shizuko Jackson, one of

Michelle's closest friends during the deployment. On the day the picture was taken, Michelle found her sitting in a chair. Jackson was low, *really* low. It had been a long day, and Jackson said it seemed like the deployment was going to go on forever, that they were never going home. "Were going to the roof," Michelle said, pulling Jackson to her feet. When they got there, Michelle turned on the CD player and Latin music boomed out of the speakers. They had taken salsa dancing lessons together in Kuwait and now Michelle gave Jackson an order: "It's time to practice!" Others drifted up to see what all the noise was about, and as the sun went down, there was dancing on the rooftop. For a little while there was an island of "normal" in a sea of war.

Chapter 8 - Then There Were Three

Charity sat on the gold-and-blue couch, the one her mother loved so much that we had to change the living room carpet to match it when we moved into the big old house in New Berlin. The cameraman fussed with lights on the far side of the coffee table, and the reporter worked to make the wireless microphones as inconspicuous as possible. When news about the deployment of the National Guard's Company B 118th got out, the family began to receive requests for interviews. The story of three sisters, three reservists, all being deployed to Iraq, was deemed newsworthy.

The Company B 118th Medical Battalion was "un-deployable." At least that's what Charity told us over and over again. They hadn't seen action since the Korean War; the unit was too small; preparations would take too long. "Were not going anywhere," she told us.

I'm not sure if Charity really believed what she was telling us or if she just believed we needed to hear it. She had witnessed the emotional wear and tear Rachel and Michelle's deployment had caused, and she didn't want to give us anything else to worry about. But now she sat with orders in hand, telling the viewing public she was ready to do her part. She was going to Iraq. The orders didn't say she was going to Iraq. In typical military fashion, the orders were vague. She was going to the "near east."

Charity sent an e-mail update to friends and family:

I just got word that my unit is being deployed. My active duty begins December 7th of next month. I should still be in Wisconsin for about a week after that. My unit will then fly to Fort Drum, New York, where we will spend a short period preparing for our overseas mission. We will meet up with the rest of our Medical Battalion and from Fort Drum we will fly overseas. I speculate our first stop will be in Kuwait where we will receive our vehicles and medical equipment and from there convoy to Iraq. We will be in Iraq for at least a year. They are telling us we will be gone for 18 to 24 months, so that is what I am preparing myself for.

As you can imagine I have many mixed emotions right now. I would ask that you please continue to pray for my sisters overseas and my family.

Not long after Charity wrote her e-mail, another e-mail would be sent to the friends-and-family distribution list, this time by Rachel, explaining that she and Michelle were eligible for leave and that they might be coming home in December. We were ecstatic. But, as if to remind us that there was still a very real war going on, the e-mail went on to describe a massive operation involving the 32nd MPs:

> … Last week we conducted raids that involved nearly every military battalion in Baghdad. We hit nearly every house in about a ten mile area, the area, that we believed, was housing one of the largest terrorist cells currently in operation. The raids took nearly ten hours and were performed in cooperation with at least twenty other companies. It was incredible. Nearly every block in our grid of operation was secured by some branch of the army. We also had at least eighteen armed Blackhawk choppers providing air support, over forty tanks patrolling, just as a show of force, and military boats patrolling every inch of the river bordering our search area. MP companies performed the actual raids with security support provided by infantry companies. It was one of the most massive operations conducted since the major conflict was declared "over."

> To top all of this off, CNN decided to follow us around. Apparently "people" (whoever that is) are concerned that Iraqi women are being treated abusively by male soldiers. This is absolutely absurd. Male soldiers are not allowed to touch the women. They can't so much as wave a metal detector wand in front of them. ALL searches of females are performed by female soldiers. Military teams were modified at the start of the war to include at least one female. If there aren't enough female soldiers, we're provided with a trained female translator who performs the searches. CNN could not have picked a more stressful night to investigate the issue!

> The raids were, by most definitions, successful. We uncovered a variety of illegal weapons, ammo, RPGs

(rocket propelled grenades) and the like. We did have one especially disturbing and groundbreaking find. We came upon a run-down house that appeared to be inhabited but, upon entry, the house was empty. It looked as though someone had just run out a back door. ... What we found was actually very scary. There was no furniture but a desk and a chair. The desk was covered in Top Secret military documents. There were a large number of books on military customs, uniform wear, customs and courtesies, and a couple of military uniforms hanging in the corner with rank and name tapes on them. We found stolen military IDs and passes that gave the user access to nearly any of our secure areas! And guard schedules with shift times and personnel rotations. There was a wide variety of weapons and ammo. A blanket covered a large pile of mortar rounds stashed in a corner along with a book on how to aim them based on degrees and distance of target. (Mortars are an exact science; if aimed correctly, mortars can hit a target up to three miles away.)

The raids were primarily a show of force in response to the recent increase in mortar attacks on US forces. But possibly most disturbing of all, we found a large stack of letters from contacts in the US. The letters contained a variety of highly classified, sensitive information. The letters were from over ten different cities including NY and Chicago. We confiscated all of it but, without a suspect to go with the items, confiscation alone was hardly reassuring. It was a *huge* find and its implications were/are terrifying. It has, however, helped us to realize just what we are dealing with and we have taken counter measures in our security procedures.

Right now we are busy with patrols and moving preparations. We will be moving our entire base camp to the opposite side of the city in January. Supposedly the new site is safer and more secure. The commander swears that once we hit ground in the new camp, it will mark the first of our last 90 days here. I would love to get excited about that, but if there is one thing I've learned, it's that *he lies*!! :) I know it's not his fault, that plans change, but I wish he wouldn't tell us things that he wasn't sure about. I have so much that I want to tell you all about, but I will save it for when I get home in the next few weeks. (Wow, it feels good to write that!)

Chapter 9 - Fifteen Days

When Charity got word that she would be deployed, Yami, the same reporter who had noticed the family at the sendoff for the 32nd MPs, came out to do a story. This was the first of several local interviews and news articles about the three sisters, all in the National Guard, serving together in Iraq. It seemed to capture the public's imagination.

The Wisconsin National Guard arranged for a priority leave. The logic was that otherwise these sisters may not see each other for a long while. Iraq is a big country, and there was no guarantee that the sisters would be stationed in the same vicinity, so it was possible that they might not see each other again for eighteen to twenty-four months

So at the same time we were reeling from the news that Charity's "non-deployable" unit was being activated and sent to Iraq, we were learning that our other two daughters, who had left us eight months earlier, were coming home on fifteen days of leave. Charity was shipping out the following week, but they would have several days together, and Michelle and Rachel would be home for fifteen glorious days.

Getting out of Iraq and back to the U.S. was not a straightforward trip. Rachel and Michelle had to wait for available transportation, and that could take many different forms. "We might come through Kuwait or we might come through Germany or we might fly on a military transport back to a base in the U.S." In the end, they took commercial transportation back to the States. We didn't know exactly when they would get in and the waiting was nearly unbearable. Rachel called late Saturday night and explained that the next flight to Milwaukee would arrive sometime late Sunday, but she called back a few hours later. "We can catch a flight to O'Hare; it doesn't get in until midnight. What should we do?"

There was no question in my mind. O'Hare was only ninety miles away, and if they could catch that flight, they would be arriving almost a full day earlier. "Take the flight!" I nearly shouted into the phone. We all wanted to meet them at the airport, but we had recently sold the family van and settled for two compact cars. They would both have duffel bags, and the reality was that unless we took two cars, I would have to pick them up alone. I left Lori and Mark and headed for

O'Hare giddy, with anticipation. There was no traffic on that crisp December night. I circled the baggage claim area looking to see if they were waiting at the curb, but there was no sign of them. I parked the car in short-term parking and went into the deserted baggage claim area and found one lone airline worker behind a counter. "Have you seen two soldiers—two female soldiers?"

"They said they were going to the other terminal to get something to eat. You should go up the stairs and take the tram."

I ran up the escalator wondering how I was going to find them, but when I got to the top, I turn the corner and there they were. "*Daddy!*" they sang out in unison, and I grabbed both of them at the same time and locked them in a fierce hug. And as I did, all of the pent-up fear and worry came out of me and I cried without reservation. We held that embrace for a long time, and by the time we were done, we were all in tears. It was just so good to be together again.

We grabbed their things and made our way to the car. On the way out, we thanked the lone baggage claim agent who not only watched Rachel and Michelle's bags but gave them a kit with toiletries so they could freshen up.

I was nearly out of gas and I needed to refuel before we got on the toll way. As we took the frontage road to the gas station, Michelle said, "I can't believe how clean the air smells! The air in Baghdad always smells like garbage or sewage." I watched the shocked expressions on their faces as we walked into the well-stocked convenience store to pay for the gas. "You forget what it's like in the U.S.," Rachel said. "You can find anything you need on every corner in America." There wasn't a quiet moment during the drive north; we stuffed as many words as we could into that ninety-minute drive, making up for lost time.

I was nearly 2:00 a.m. when we arrived at the house, and Lori had fallen asleep on the small day bed in the upstairs study. She stirred when we came in and sprang up just as the girls were coming up the stairs. We all stood in the narrow hallway as Lori clung to her daughters and cried. Mark emerged from his room as the commotion grew, and the scene was repeated as the siblings were reunited. We ended up sitting on the study floor listening to Rachel and Michelle's stories until 4:00 a.m. They took gifts out of their duffel bags and explained where they had gotten each of them: paintings, scarves, and clothing. We talked until we couldn't keep our eyes open, and then Michelle and Rachel flopped down on the little double bed in what used to be Rachel's bedroom, succumbing to the exhaustion brought on by their journey.

Charity shared a flat with her brother Tim, and we had not succeeding in reaching her to tell her that her sisters had arrived early. After she picked up her messages early that morning, she rushed over to the house at 6:00 a.m., bursting into the bedroom where her sisters were sleeping, diving between them on the bed. The commotion woke everyone in the house and we all assembled at the bedroom door, laughing at the sight of the three of them piled together on the small bed. They lay there, shoulder-to-shoulder, for a long time just talking. Lori and I drifted downstairs, giving them their space but smiling at the sound of their chatter. The sound of the three of them together again was like music to our ears.

Charity came down stairs and said, "I have to report to the armory by eight, but the commander is allowing anyone that wants to, to go to a church service that's being held at Elmbrook church. It's part of the sendoff." Michelle and Rachel rallied, showering and changing into clean uniforms—desert BDUs (battle dress uniforms,) and then we all went to church. We spotted the soldiers of the 118th and their family members sitting together in a section of the large auditorium, and we added our family to their numbers. Some of the local television stations were there to cover the sendoff and when word got out that the Witmer sisters were in the service, one reporter brought her cameraman in to the auditorium in the middle of the service and began taking shots of the family.

As we gathered in the foyer, after the service we heard someone say, "Hey, Witmer! How'd you get your desert uniform?" Charity's unit was dressed in green uniforms. The soldier had approached Michelle, assuming it was Charity. The twin sisters, both in uniform, would generate double-takes throughout the morning.

We lingered, as our daughters caught up with people they hadn't seen in nearly a year, but we were very aware of the fact that the clock was running. Rachel and Michelle had fifteen days of leave, and only four of those days would overlap with Charity being in town. Her unit was leaving for Fort Drum, New York, later that week. Our first priority was to maximize their time together. We were running on fumes, but we didn't have time to catch up on our sleep.

Charity had to report back to the Armory later in the day, so we decided to squeeze in brunch before dropping her off. We called our good friends, the Glatzels, to invite them to join us at a local restaurant, but they vetoed the idea, insisting that they would cook for us, inviting us over to their home, an old Victorian frame house in the heart of downtown Waukesha.

On the way to the Glatzels, Lori's cell phone rang; it was a local columnist from the Milwaukee Journal-Sentinel; she had seen the news coverage of the church service and wanted to know if she could meet with us for an interview. The euphoria, generated by having our daughters together again, made us pushovers; we invited her to meet us at the Glatzel's house. The family picture snapped by the photographer that day was beautiful: our three daughters, all in uniform, sandwiching their mother in an embrace. It would eventually grace the front page of the *Milwaukee Journal Sentinel*.

We sat with our dear friends and ate and talked and laughed; we sang Christmas carols and we treasured every moment. Charity left to return to the Armory, and later that afternoon, Rachel and Michelle followed her to the armory where the three of them met to talk, on camera, with some of the local reporters. There seemed to be no shortage of interest from the media. It seemed everyone wanted to know about the three sisters who were being briefly reunited before heading off to the battlefield.

Their last night in town, the company commander allowed the soldiers' families to come to the hotel where 118th had gathered to spend the night. They would board buses early the next day and be transported to the airport and then travel on to Fort Drum. We jammed ourselves into Charity's hotel room: family, extended family, and friends each arriving with snacks or drinks, instinctively bringing with them some component of this impromptu going-away party. We laughed and talked until curfew. And then we formed a line to give Charity the hug that would have to last a year or more.

On Saturday morning, December 13, I awoke to the sounds of Michelle shouting something I couldn't make out. Panicked, I raced up the stairs to the sitting room to find Michelle shouting at the television. "They got him! They got him! They got Saddam!" Michelle could not contain herself. Many believed that once Saddam Hussein was captured, the insurgency would crumble and the war would be over. The prospect of peace in Iraq had Michelle literally jumping up and down. Shortly after that the phone began to ring. One of the local TV stations wanted the Witmer sisters to provide commentary as they covered the breaking news of the capture of Iraq's former president, and Michelle and Rachel provided their perspective by phone as the graphic at the bottom of the TV screen identified them as subject matter experts.

The days passed by much too quickly and Rachel and Michelle were being pulled in every direction. We had to plan family functions so that the aunts and uncles could get together and see their nieces. There were friends to see and parties to attend. The time flew by, and I struggled to find one-on-one time with my girls. I took Rachel to lunch but Michelle was so busy, I settled on finding time to take her out for coffee. As we sat at Starbucks sipping our lattes, I began to get emotional. I told Michelle how hard the last year had been, and I confessed that I worried about her constantly. "You have to come home safe; if I lost you I would be in *hell*." We both broke down, giving up any pretense of being strong. She reached across the table, held both my hands, and said, "I will, Dad, I promise. I *promise* you I'll come home.

The fifteen days passed in an instant and we found ourselves reluctantly loading the car to take Rachel and Michelle to the airport. In all the travel, shuttling, packing, and unpacking, Rachel had misplaced her airline ticket, so we left several hours early to give her plenty of time to get it replaced and allow for a long goodbye over a cup of coffee. Rachel went to the counter to make what she thought would be routine request in the age of e-tickets. The gate agent explained that in the case of military travel, the paper ticket is a voucher and the airline had to have the voucher to receive payment from the government. Even though Rachel had a seat reserved on the flight, without the paper ticket, she couldn't get on the plane. "I can sell you a ticket," the agent offered."

"How much would it be," Rachel inquired.

"Eight-hundred-ninety-seven dollars with tax," the agent replied."

Rachel was 24-years old, a soldier, and a seasoned member of the MPs; she was more than capable of working through the situation. But I went into daddy-mode. "This woman is about to get on a plane to return to Iraq to fight for our country and all that we hold dear and the best you can do is offer her a nine hundred dollar ticket for the seat she's already purchased! I want to see your supervisor." The supervisor took the same position as the ticket agent. I was about to call his patriotism into question, in a loud and dramatic way with words

I'm sure I would have regretted, when a ticket agent from another airline intervened.

"I overheard your conversation," he said politely. He looked at Rachel. "Do you have military I.D.?

"Of course," Rachel replied."

"Then we can get you back to Baltimore for seventy-nine dollars."

I wanted to hug the man. "The only problem," he continues, "is the plane is leaving in twenty-five minutes. You're going to need to hurry." The offer was a godsend, but our leisurely goodbye went out the window. As we hustled to security, once again daddy-mode kicked in, and I started asking people in the security line to step aside because my daughter needed to make a flight. When she got past the person checking IDs, I was flagging the TSA agent, pointing out my daughter, yelling to him that she needs to get through quickly if she was going to make her flight. Rachel endured the embarrassment of Dad treating her like she was ten-years old and she made her flight. The rest of us went to the airport coffee shop to sit with Michelle until she had to leave to catch her plane. And when the time finally came, we watched her walk through security. Just as we had with Rachel, we waved goodbye until she was out of sight. I can still see in my mind's eye the last time she turned and looked at me, as she walked down the concourse.

After that, something changed in me. I'd spent the preceding months in a state of high anxiety. Every morning I would wake up and carefully listen to the radio reports on the war. "A soldier was killed …" I went through my list: Was it Baghdad? Was it Military Police? Was it a woman? I clung to every detail. The daily stress wore me down, and the only comfort I had was knowing that someday soon it would all be over, that soon my daughters would be back in their own beds. When Charity's unit was called up, it was like having someone move the finish line in the middle of a marathon—tacking on another twenty miles when you thought the end was in sight. She was not scheduled to return until February of 2005. I was exhausted from months of worry; now I was faced with another fourteen months of having soldier-daughters in the war zone. I moved from anxiety to denial; I just went numb.

Chapter 10 - The End in Sight

Charity, thanks to the efforts of those who went before her, would have immediate access to the Internet, and she was able to update us almost as soon as she arrived in Baghdad.

Just wanted to quick say "hi" and see how you're doing. Baghdad is, well—Baghdad. Besides the occasional mortar round and RPG, it's actually not too bad. I haven't seen my sisters yet, but I'm hoping that I'll see them in the next week or so. Right now they are in two separate locations so it makes it a little more difficult.

I am working as the night NCO (non-commissioned officer A.K.A. Sergeant), so my schedule is pretty out of whack. They also put me in charge of mass-casualty incidents, which are a huge undertaking. We are working in about four different areas, so my company is pretty spread out. We treat all the Iraqi detainees and prisoners including *all* the high-profile ones (and I do mean *all*). We are required to put tape over our name tags on our uniforms because, apparently, the prisoners we treat have been known to take revenge on families back home in the states, which is why we also have to burn any mail with return addresses on it. It's all pretty crazy.

We have had some mortar fire since we've been here, but nothing too close.

On our convoy up, we had to stop, twice, for the night, because of sniper fire.

They also found two IEDs on the road we were traveling on. Luckily they were caught in time and disaster was averted.

That's all the news on this side of world.

Charity spent several weeks in Fort Drum and then traced her sisters' footsteps, spending time in Kuwait before making the convoy north to Baghdad. Just a few weeks before Charity sent her first e-mail from Iraq, Rachel sent her own e-mail with some good news.

> Hey, I only have a second, would you please post this on the website: Our Leadership has asked us to notify our families to stop sending packages. (This only applies to Michelle and Rachel.) This is a *really good sign*! ... The redeployment process (though it may be long) is finally beginning! There is finally a light at the end of the tunnel! Please tell everyone how much we appreciate the packages and support they have given us.

The 32nd MPs would be winding down as the Company B 118th Medical Battalion was ramping up. Charity was stationed near Baghdad International Airport; Rachel and Michelle were near the heart of Baghdad, some twenty miles away. But twenty miles might as well be a thousand when it's in the middle of a war zone. We had no idea if our daughters would ever be able to see each other when they were in country. Not only would they have to find secure transportation, but their days off would have to be aligned. Three months after our daughters last saw each other, the leadership of both companies worked to make a reunion possible. In the middle of March, we received an e-mail, from Charity.

> Well, I was able to see Shelly and Rae together for the first time this weekend. I was supposed to stay for two nights but a mission came up and I had to leave after the first night.

A few days later, Charity posted pictures of the Baghdad reunion on the family website: three smiling soldiers, all in desert BDUs, with the streets of Baghdad as their backdrop. In one picture, the three of them are all holding puppies. A few months earlier, a three-legged street dog, began hanging around the camp. The soldiers nicknamed her "Tripod," and Michelle began tending to the dog. Tripod had produced a litter of puppies, and the picture was snapped as Michelle was proudly showing off Tripod's offspring with her sisters. In hindsight, that time together in Baghdad would be precious. It would be the last time they were together.

Charity's company was on the move. Half of the unit was deployed to Babylon, leaving Charity and twelve others to cover the duties at BIAP. Charity ran sick call every morning and tended to the needs of those who presented themselves for treatment. The plan was to reunite the unit in Babylon in a little over a month. In the meantime, Charity got her own room, a welcome change from a tent with twenty-nine roommates.

On April 9th, a couple weeks after their Baghdad reunion, Charity got this e-mail from Michelle:

Hey Sweetie Bear,

Life here has been very crazy the last week or so. About five days ago at ten at night our Platoon Sergeant starts running into our rooms saying that the Baghdad police stations are getting overrun and there are riots all over the city. We have to hurry and get all our shit on and go take care of the situation. We have been virtually living at the police stations. We are there twenty-four hours a day and this is the first time I've gotten back to Mustang base in three days and I have to leave again at midnight to go back out. The police stations are so nasty and dirty and it sucks to be there for so long. In the meantime were getting attacked almost nightly with RPGs, mortars and small arms fire. Rachel's station, in Al Adameyhia, got the worst of it. I was really afraid for her over in that area. Well I gotta run. I have a lot of catching up to do.

Charity, please pray for us; this is some scary shit. Some of the worst I've seen since I've been here. I gotta get some sleep. Hopefully by next week this will all be over.

Love you forever,

Shelly

Michelle had always been a deeply empathetic and intuitive person; knowing that, two things jumped out at me when Charity shared this e-mail with me a few weeks later.

"Love you forever." It was a line from a children's book of the same title, one we had read to our children many times when they were little. It begins with a mother holding her baby son, rocking him and singing, "I'll love you forever, I'll love you for always, as long as I'm living, my baby you'll be." The story advances until the mother is in the final stages of her life and ends with the now-adult son holding his tiny, frail mother in his arms as he sings, "I'll love you forever, I'll love you for always, as long as I'm living, my mother you'll be." Michelle knew that the phrase would convey strong emotion to Charity, the written equivalent of a long embrace. "Shelly" was the nickname only those closest to her were entitled to use. Michelle reminded Charity of this by signing off, not as Michelle, but as Shelly.

Rachel felt the need to watch out for Michelle; that's what big sisters do. Michelle was barely twenty. Rachel had four years on her, and though she was smaller than Michelle, she could still take her in a fair fight, a fact she had proven the last time they were home, on leave, by pinning her down on the kitchen floor.

Rachel and Michelle's squads had assembled for midnight chow in the Green Zone, an area of Baghdad containing buildings that were once Saddam Hussein's palaces but now served as Collation Headquarters and home for the 32nd MPs. The squads were forming their convoys, getting ready to roll out to their assigned police stations. Like always, Rachel took the gunner seat. That's the way they did it in First Platoon. Each member of the squad had a specific job. Michelle would split her time between driving and gunning.

By now the big machine gun felt natural in her hands. She could lay down 750 rounds per minute with this turret-mounted M-249. The insurgents understood how deadly this gun was and just turning it in the direction of the enemy was often enough to make them turn and run. The obvious downside of being in the turret was being the most exposed member of the squad.

Rachel looked up and noticed that Michelle was also in the turret of her Humvee. An odd feeling came over her and she wondered why Michelle was in the turret; she usually drove. Rachel was overcome with a sudden urge to leave her vehicle and embrace her sister. But she shook it off as a bad case of nerves and got ready to head out.

Chapter 11 - The Knock

Six vehicles exited the Green Zone through Assassin's Gate; one squad turned right, across the Tigress River, toward Al A'zamiyah, the other continued north. Just minutes later, high-caliber bullets rained down on the northbound convoy. An RPG landed on the curb as an explosion crippled the lead vehicle. The lead vehicle swerved hard to the right. *"Get going! Get going!"* the driver of the second vehicle shouted as he rammed the lead vehicle, forcing it ahead, trying to move both vehicles out of the kill zone.

The doorbell rang at 7:35 on Friday evening; Lori and I were home alone. Mark, the only one of our children living at home, was at gymnastics practice. I was planning to go to a movie with my friend, Joe; he would be meeting me at the house. I was not expecting him until eight, so when the doorbell rang I thought he had decided to come a little early.

I was talking to my sister on the phone when the bell rang, so Lori answered the door. I heard Lori saying something and then I realized she was saying "No! No! No!" over and over again. I dropped the phone and ran to the door. A man in uniform stood in the doorway. I looked at his face and it registered. Two more uniforms stood behind him. Lori's hands were cradling her forehead; she kept saying, "No! No!" but now it was like a rebuke, like she was trying to order them away from our door.

At that moment, things begin to happen in slow motion. I realize why they are here. I begin to bargain in my mind, "Please God let it be an injury ..." But I know better. They call if your soldier is injured. *There is only one reason they come to your door.*

Tracer bullets flecked the night sky. The lieutenant looked up through the hatch; his gunner, a bright young woman, with so much to live for, was slumped forward, looking down. He took her in his arms, placed her across the back seat, and began CPR as the convoy pushed through the three-block-long ambush.

I was talking to my sister on the phone when the bell rang; when I heard Lori, saying "No! No!" I didn't drop the phone, I threw it. It took me hours to remember that I was in the middle of a conversation when I threw the phone down—hours before it even registered that my sister would be concerned.

There were three of them in Class A uniforms: forest green, brass buttons, medals and insignias precisely placed, black shoes shined to a high luster. They were standing in my living room, on my dark blue carpet, holding their hats.

There is only one reason they come to your door.

I didn't intend to shout it; it just came out that way. *"Who?* We have three daughters in Iraq! *WHO?"*

The convoy crossed the Tigris River, and after reaching the relative safety of a field artillery base, they continued CPR on their gunner. The lieutenant was puzzled. She had been wounded in the shoulder; there was very little bleeding, but she was not breathing. But then they saw the blood around her mouth. They continued CPR as they struggled to understand her injuries. For a moment, they wrestled with whether they should stay and support the other vehicles, conceding that she was gone, or break away and rush her to the hospital. Not ready to give up on the resuscitation effort, they left the convoy. Hospital personnel continued to try and revive her, but it was hopeless. The bullet, which hit her in the shoulder, passed through her heart, stopping it almost instantly.

The sun was streaming in the sunroom windows. It had been a beautiful spring day, one that should have faded, peacefully, into twilight. But then they came to our door.

It was 7:35 when Lori began saying, *"No! No! No!"*

It was 7:35 when I threw down the phone and ran to the door.

It was 7:35 when I shouted, *"Who?"* when the General, flanked by a Chaplin and a Causality Officer, said "Mr. and Mrs. Witmer, the Wisconsin National Guard regrets to inform you . . ."

It was 7:35 when he said her name, when, after what seemed like an eternity, he said ". . . Michelle Witmer was killed in action."

Rachel heard chatter on the radio below, but she couldn't make it out. "Witmer; they want you back at Mustang Base." The statement didn't really register. Turn back? Now? They were almost to Al Adamia. She argued, calling down from the turret, "Are you sure? What's going on? Why do they need *me?*"

"Your sister's been hurt; nothing serious."

"Nothing serious" had never been a reason to turnaround.

As Rachel's vehicle headed back to base, it started to sink in. They were holding back. If they wanted her back at Mustang Base, then Michelle's injuries were serious. It had to be life-and-death. Rachel was prepared for bad news when she approached her commander, but she was not prepared to hear what came out his mouth, "She didn't make it."

"*She didn't make it?*" Rachel echoed in disbelief.

My daughter's name, coming out of the General's mouth has the power of a blow to the head. I drop to my knees. Someone speaks to me. They seem far away. They ask if there's anyone they should call.

I keep saying, "*NO! NO! NO!*" over and over again.

I am pounding the floor with my fist, pounding the white tile of the sun room floor. I installed this floor; worked on it for hours; smoothing in the blue grout that frames each square. Michelle told me what I nice job I had done. Now I hate this tile. I want to smash it! Smash it into a million pieces, this ridiculous tile that Michelle will never see again and I pound on it over and over again with my fist.

Lori is somewhere close by; I can hear her sobs. From somewhere I hear her voice say over and over again, "What are we gonna do?" The uniforms try to console me. I know words are coming out of their mouths, but I don't hear them. My stomach knots up and my throat aches and I begin to feel sick. I put my hand to my chest and panic registers on the faces of the uniforms. They ask me if I am on any medication. They worry that I might need a doctor. I move to the bathroom, off the kitchen, and stand over the toilet with the dry heaves.

I cry until my eyes are nearly swollen shut. When I look at the clock, only minutes have passed. Hours and hours of pain have somehow been compressed into a few minutes. It's as if I'm trapped in this horrible moment.

My friend Joe is supposed to be on his way. He should be here any minute. The uniform people are trying to call him.

My sister.

"Someone should call my sister. She'll wonder why I dropped the phone." The uniform people are dialing numbers.

Tim.

"Call my son Tim. Find him. He should be here."

"What about Mark? Did you reach him?"

"Do Rachel and Charity know?"

My head hurts. I cry some more, I heave some more. The clock refuses to move.

"Where are my friends?"

"Where's my sister?"

"Why is no one here yet?"

"Did you find Tim? Is he coming?"

I want these uniforms to leave. I want someone to tell me it was all a mistake.

After what seems like an eternity, Tim comes. We cry together, but I can't make out what is happening around me. Then my sister comes and speaks to me.

"Are you sure? *Make* them check again! This could be a mistake."

"Who else should we call?"

Rachel will call but no one is sure when. The uniforms help me call the rest of my family, eight brothers and sisters. Some I can talk to and some I can't. I have brief moments where I feel the need to do something. Look up a phone number. Make a suggestion about who to call next. And then I'm sucked back into the blackness. My forehead feels like someone hit it with a baseball bat.

I'm not sure when the uniforms leave. Each one tells me their name, each one leaves a card. One is a woman; the other two are men. A General? A Chaplin? A Causality Officer?

Slowly friends and family arrive at the house. I go to the basement and drag out a trunk of family photos and put it down in the middle of the kitchen floor. Unprompted, we all start to go through the massive pile of unsorted pictures, mining for Michelle, pulling out memories. We do this for hours as people come and go.

At 4:00 a.m., I sit down in a recliner. I doze, but wake up at 6:00 a.m. I enjoy just a few minutes of amnesia before it comes back to me. Then the crying starts again and I can't stop it; it possesses me, it goes on and on. It hurts to cry. My forehead aches, and when I sob, my whole body hurts; but I can do nothing else.

Rachel's next mission would be the hardest of her life. She would travel the fourteen miles across town to BIAP to deliver the news to Charity. It was decided that they would wait until morning, judging that it was better to let Charity have one last night of sleep untainted by this memory. Only a twin can understand what it's like to be one-of-two and two-who-are-one. When Charity received the news, she reflected the depth of that unique bond; it was if someone had cut-off a piece of her. Anger, hurt, rage and sorrow erupted from her, all in the same moment. The Chaplin, sent to comfort her was on a fool's errand. She was beyond consoling as she repeated the same question, over and over again: *Why?*

Chapter 12 - Holy Saturday

It didn't register that it was Holy Saturday, or that it had been Good Friday when they knocked on our door. We had received two very brief phone calls, from Rachel and Charity, in the wee hours of the morning, and now we waited for word that they were on a plane, headed home.

The house was quiet when the phone rang. It was General Jeremiah Denson of the Wisconsin National Guard. It registered that he was one of the soldiers that came to our door the night before. He was checking in with us. He wanted to know if there was anything we need. I asked him about Rachel and Charity.

"If I understood you correctly, last night, you told me they would not have to go back to Iraq."

Whether he said this or whether I simply refused to hear anything else, I can't tell. I certainly asked the question, and I thought he had given me the answer I wanted to hear.

He told me that Rachel was within 90 days of the end of her tour of duty and that under the circumstances, Army regulations allowed her to stay stateside. But then he told me that according to those same Army regulations, Charity would be required to return to Iraq and complete her tour of duty after fifteen days of emergency leave. I was stunned. I stammered out a "thank you" and hung up.

"According to regulations," I turned these words over and over in my mind, "Charity will have to return to Iraq … according to regulations."

The next call we received was from Iraq. The voice on the other end of the phone explained that arrangements had been made and that Rachel and Charity would be accompanying Michelle's body back to the United States. They also explained that Michelle's body would need to remain in Baltimore until a complete autopsy could be performed. It was a necessary part of the "homicide investigation." But Rachel and Charity will be free to travel on to Wisconsin to be with family. "Baghdad International Airport is taking mortar fire and all planes are grounded until the area can be secured," the official explained. "We'll let you know when they get in the air."

About 45 minutes later, the phone rang again. It was the General. "Mr. Witmer, we expect that there will be a great deal of interest in this story. There may be as many as twenty media organizations in front of your house once we release the statement this afternoon." He told me the National Guard had public-relations officers who could help us prepare a statement and that they could send someone to the house so we wouldn't have to talk to the press. Then he gave me his number.

It didn't sink in. I didn't really understand what he was telling me. Again, I thanked the General and hung up. And again, I turned his words over in my mind, "twenty media organizations … public interest … PR people."

Slowly, I began to feel the anger. Charity must return to Baghdad. My family has given the ultimate sacrifice, but that wasn't enough, Charity had to return to complete her tour in the same "hostile fire zone" where Michelle lost her life. A twin, grieving the loss of her twin, must go back to war and carry on like it never happened. A family with a hole blown through it must heal seven thousand miles apart. It was Army regulations.

I dialed the General's number. He answers and I start slow, like a freight train leaving the yard, gradually picking up speed. "Let me see if I understand this: according to Army regulations, Charity is required to return to Baghdad to complete her tour."

"That's right."

"You've also told me that twenty different media organizations will be camping on my front lawn."

"That's correct," he replied.

I abandoned what little restraint I was clinging to and fired back, "This is the way it is; either you find a way to make sure my daughters stay stateside or I will stand in front of all those cameras and *I promise you I will make a scene!* Don't quote army regulations to me! I've lost one daughter, I will *not* lose another. *You need to fix this!*"

The General tried to calm me down. You don't want to do that. It won't help. It will have no impact on the decision-making process. It will unleash a media firestorm that will overwhelm your family and only add to your burden. He assured me that the Wisconsin National Guard was pulling for us, that they wanted to help, that even though the decision about where Charity was deployed was not within their control, he would take the matter to the Pentagon first thing on Monday morning.

My mind was racing. Stereotypes of government bureaucracy sprang to mind as I imagined the request sitting on some faceless bureaucrat's desk while Charity's fifteen days of leave slipped away. I thought about what it would be like if I had to watch Charity board a plane for Iraq. I didn't know this man, so how could I leave my daughter's fate in his hands. "We won't need your help" I tell him, "and you won't need to send anyone over. We'll take care of this ourselves," I declare, as I try to get my anger under control.

Later that day, we would learn the 32nd MPs tour of duty had been extended. The day after the company lost one of its own, they got the news that their tour had been extended. This meant that Rachel was no longer near the finish line. She, too, would have to go back to Iraq. Out of the fog of grief came a fierce energy—a primal need to protect our daughters; it wasn't rational, it wasn't reasonable, and it wasn't patient. Asking Rachel and Charity how they felt about it never even crossed our minds. All we knew was that we had lost Michelle and that now we needed Rachel and Charity to be safe.

In that moment, it became our mission. We had no idea how to go about it, but if the media could help us get our message out, "that we had given enough and that our surviving daughters should be allowed reassignment," so be it.

We opened the door to the public. And we unleashed everything that comes with being in the public eye. The General's words would prove to be prophetic. We would receive hate mail. We would become the subject of opinion polls. We would become the topic-of-the-day on local drive-time talk radio. We did unleash a firestorm. But we would have gladly faced the gates of hell if it meant protecting Rachel and Charity.

Lori and I had no plan. There was no instruction book or manual to guide us, but our determination to make sure that our surviving daughters could be reassigned drove us into uncharted waters. We pushed forward, trying to figure it out as we went along. As a result, we took on the biggest project of our lives at a time when we should have been consoling one another and planning our daughter's funeral.

We started by calling our U.S. congressman and senators. We left messages on machines or with answering services, briefly explaining our plight, leaving contact information. Then we sat down at the computer and began to compose letters. Michelle had been killed less than twenty-four hours earlier, and now we were trying to decide what salutation to use when writing to a senator.

There had been a small stream of visitors as word of Michelle's death spread, and now several friends volunteered to help us with our mission: to get assurances that Rachel and Charity would be reassigned out of harm's way. By late that afternoon, all three of our computers were in use. We were combing the Internet for addresses of state and federal officials, working on letters to politicians, and drafting our statement to the press—the statement we decided we could write without the help of the Wisconsin National Guard.

On Saturday afternoon, the Army released a brief statement explaining that "Michelle Witmer, of New Berlin, Wisconsin, was killed in Baghdad, Iraq, in an incident involving an IED and small weapons fire." That's when the phone began to ring.

Our friends shifted to phone duty. The local stations wanted an interview. The newspaper wanted a statement. We couldn't ignore these calls; we knew we needed the help of these journalists to get our message out, to make our request visible to someone with the authority to do something about it. Our short-term strategy was to take down the contact information and try and sort it out later. We started with scrawling notes on scraps of paper, but the messages quickly piled up and we struggled to stay organized. We moved to a note pad. By the end of week, we would progress to a three-ring binder with dividers.

We offered no comment to the reporters who called, but we let them know that there would be a press conference at 3:00 p.m. on Easter Sunday. For the most part, the journalists were respectful, and when we let them know a statement was forthcoming they gave us our space, at least in the beginning.

We worked for hours on the statement, going back and forth on the wording. We had to strike a balance. The public needed to know how much we respected the Army National Guard and our daughter's service, but they we also needed to understand our dilemma. And somewhere, in that audience, we reasoned, would be someone who could do something about it.

Slowly, a strategy came together. Not that we were smart enough to come up with it on our own. Joan Apt, a family friend, from our years in Minnesota, seemed to materialize out of thin air. I'm not sure when she arrived, but when she did, she rolled up her sleeves and went to work. What we didn't know was that Joni had worked in public relations for the Archdiocese of Minneapolis. It was Joni who answered the door when reporters knocked. Most, she politely turned away, explaining that we would be holding a press conference, but some she talked to, sensing that they could help us understand how to best navigate this confusing road.

Jim, a producer from one of the major networks, was one of the people Joni invited into our living room, and he was the one who offered up a strategy. "If you want to get your message out without dealing with dozens of reporters, you should make a statement to the Associated Press." He reasoned that we could then refer all other print journalists to that statement. "And you should accept the request for an interview from the *Today Show*, because the White House monitors the program."

When I spoke to the General, I had threatened to make a scene, but in reality, Lori and I had neither the desire nor the energy to face the cameras. An angry, tearful statement, given by grieving parents would dishonor Michelle's memory and our daughters' service; we couldn't do that. We decided that we would stay in the house and that Joni would act as our spokesperson. She would read the words we had labored over for hours, words that were meant to respectfully convey our message. That we, as a family, had given enough and that the Army should facilitate the reassignment of our daughters.

Shortly before 3:00 p.m., copies of the statement were distributed to the crowd of reporters on our front lawn, and then Joni walked out to the collection of microphone stands. Shutters clicked, spotlights came to life, and satellite trucks, fed by a tangle of cables that snaked across our lawn, idled in the background. She read our words in a clear, steady voice, delivering the statement like the professional she was, and then declined to answer questions. Shortly after the press conference, I found the message from the AP and returned the call, giving the reporter a phone interview. Then we returned the call from the *Today Show* producer and agreed to be interviewed Monday morning. Everything was on track until Rachel called.

Fifty-two hours after Michelle was killed, all three of my daughters were back on U.S. soil. Rachel called us from her hotel room on Sunday night to let us know they were in the States, that they would be arriving home sometime late Monday morning.

I started gushing about all the work we had been doing to make sure they could be reassigned. I was going on and on when Rachel politely and firmly interrupted, "Dad. You need to listen. I appreciate all you're trying to do and I understand why you're doing it, but it's not your decision to make. And in any case," she explained, "we have to respect the chain of command; there's a way these things need to be handled." I tried to argue with her, but she stopped me again, "Dad, we want to be with our family more than anything else in the world, but the problem is we have two families now. Our family in Wisconsin and the people we serve with in Iraq. You can't just walk away from the people who had your back, people who would take a bullet for you," she explained. "Let's not talk about this now," she said, "let's just get Michelle home. Let's just get through the funeral."

I remember exactly where I was when I we had this conversation; I remember which phone I was on and where I was standing in the room. As a father, every fiber of my being wanted to protect my girls. Every part of me wanted to make sure the nightmare would be over, that there would be no more long days wondering if my girls were okay—if they had made it through another day. But the reality hit me like a bucket of cold water. I was not in control here. In fact, I had made a mess of things. A sick feeling came over me when I realized that they might be going back and that it might be because they wanted to go back. Then a wave of exhaustion swept over me.

Chapter 13 - In the Spotlight

Shortly before Rachel's call, I had been on the phone with the *Today Show* producers walking them through our story: three daughters in Baghdad, one killed in action, two more still assigned to the war zone—the Army National Guard informing us that they would have to go back to Iraq after the funeral leave. The producer told us a car would be sent to pick us up at 5:45 a.m. It would take us to a hotel, a few miles away, where a "remote" had been setup. Our live interview, with the *Today Show* co-host Katie Couric was scheduled to lead off the second half-hour.

We got up at 4:00 a.m. to get ready for the interview. We were exhausted, we were sick with grief, and we had gotten way ahead of our daughters in asking that they be reassigned. "Should we cancel the interview?" I asked Lori.

"Even if it isn't our decision to make, they should still have the option of reassignment," she contended. But with Rachel's words ringing in my ears, it would be a very different interview than the one I had imagined.

Lori and I sat side-by-side under bright lights in front of a portable backdrop as we were wired for sound in the hotel room suite that had been converted into a temporary studio. Cables snaked their way out of the first-floor room to a satellite truck. Producers watched video feeds in the adjoining room on a bank of monitors. The room seemed to be jammed with technical people.

As they prepped us for the interview, I could hear the *Today Show* audio in the background. They were teasing our story as "A modern day 'Saving Private Ryan.'" My stomach knotted as I heard, "… now Michelle's grieving parents are trying to get their other two daughters home from Iraq for good. We'll have an interview with them in just a few minutes."

The activity continued all around us as we waited for our cue. Lighting was adjusted, microphones were checked, and camera angles were fine tuned. We knew the drill. We had been in front of the cameras several times as local television stations covered the story of our three daughters, all serving in Iraq together.

"Five minutes"

The activity around us had peaked and now the room became quiet. We watched the commercial break on the monitor and then the *Today Show* theme accompanied the show's graphic.

Katie Couric faced the camera and said, "A Wisconsin couple is in mourning today after their twenty-year-old daughter was killed in Iraq. Now, just like in 'Saving Private Ryan,' they're trying to keep their two other daughters, serving there, out of harm's way. NBC's Kevin Tibbles reports."

The screen filled with pictures of Rachel, Charity, and Michelle, most of them taken when Rachel and Michelle were home on leave four months earlier. There had been plenty of material to choose from. Our family had been in the news, off and on, for over a year. Local interest in the story of the family with three daughters serving in Iraq was high. We'd had many requests for interviews and had accepted all of them. Shortly before our daughters deployed, we discussed it, and we felt if our family's story could help bring attention to the sacrifices made by our service men and women and their families, it was well worth the intrusion.

Most reporters were respectful, but some did intrude. In December, when the CO (commanding officer) of Charity's unit invited his soldiers and their families to attend church with him for what would be their final Sunday in town, a reporter and cameraman entered the sanctuary, marching down the main aisle mid-service, filming close-ups of the girls as we sat in church. The footage from that church service now filled the screen as an unseen announcer narrated, *"She was just twenty years old. SPC Michelle Witmer of New Berlin, Wisconsin, one of three sisters all serving in Iraq."*

Now footage of our press conference, the day before, was being shown. The sound bite was Joni reading the statement, "Michelle believed in her mission and she made a real difference in the lives of many people."

"Witmer was killed Friday, after her humvee came under attack," the announcer continued. As more images, of Michelle filled the screen, *"She had been in Iraq for over a year. Family and friends are now pleading with the National Guard to remove her sisters from harm's way."*

At first, I was surprised when major media outlets got it wrong; I always assumed there was rigorous fact checking before a story aired.

But in the weeks to come, I would learn that errors in reporting were common. Michelle and Rachel had been *deployed* over a year at the time she was killed, but they had been in Iraq about ten months. It took about six weeks to prepare the unit and another month in Kuwait to acclimate before they went on to Iraq.

The images reverted to the news conference as Joan said, "We have appealed to the Army National Guard to grant whatever exceptions are necessary to make sure Rachel and Charity are not returned to Iraq. "

The Announcer continued as a clip from the movie '*Saving Private Ryan*' was shown; it's the scene where the grief-stricken mother of the Ryan boys collapses on the porch: *"There is a rule in the military named for the Sullivan Brothers that prohibits family members from serving side-by-side after all five Sullivan Brothers were killed at sea and in the movie,* 'Saving Private Ryan' *the military notifies a Midwestern mother that three of her four sons are dead. It's a scene a Wisconsin family doesn't want repeated."*

The Sullivan rule—it had been mentioned to us over and over again in the last few days. Here it was again, tossed around like it was bona fide military operating policy. As best we could tell from online searches, it was a relic of history that applied specifically to the Navy and family members serving on the same ship. Everyone knew about it, but no one could come up with an actual copy or tell us if the rule was in any way relevant to our situation.

Back to our front-lawn news conference, as Joni says, "We trust that those in charge of making such a decision will realize that we have already sacrificed enough and that our family must not be asked to bear such an impossible burden."

This is the sound bite that went around the world. It seemed to be included in every story we saw, in every article we read. It would become fodder for radio talk-show hosts and TV surveys:

"Should the Witmer sisters return to Iraq?"

"Was it unpatriotic to make a public appeal?"

The lead-in piece continued, *"Before leaving for Iraq, Michelle Witmer said that she was prepared to serve."* And there she was, Michelle: her image, her words, her voice filling the screen. The clip was from February 2003. Michelle had happened upon a gathering at the university of Wisconsin–Milwaukee, a peace rally. The demonstration consisted of hundreds of "striking" students who had gathered in the student union. At the center of the crowd were a group of students playing drums, dancing, and carrying banners. A reporter from one of the local TV stations was interviewing one of the rally leaders.

Growing up, Michelle had struggled with her identity. She always felt like the child without a gift, that she had been passed over when God was handing out special talent. Rachel could sing and acted professionally as a child. Tim was also a child actor, and his teachers identified him as "gifted and talented." Charity was enrolled in the same accelerated learning program as Tim, and Mark was recognized for his athletic ability, eventually going on to earn a spot on the University of Minnesota's gymnastics team.

Michelle did well in school, but she was not in the "gifted club." She was athletic and played team sports, but she did not stand out. She could act and she was involved in drama, but the family's move from Minneapolis to Milwaukee closed the door on any serious acting opportunities. She always felt she walked in the shadow of her siblings.

In high school, she began to find her place in the world. She joined the debate team and signed up for a trip to Washington, D.C. She volunteered to help candidate George W. Bush at a rally in Waukesha, Wisconsin, documenting the occasion by having her picture taken with the future president of the United States. She was planning to study journalism. She wanted to be involved in her world. She wanted to make a difference.

Her gift, the gift she didn't see, was compassion. Michelle was deeply loyal and empathetic. When she cared about something or someone, she cared until it hurt.

And as she took in the dancing protestors, her passion, her zeal, her *gift*, manifested. She walked up to the reporter covering the story and asked, "Would you like another perspective?"

She explained that she respected the rights of these students to assemble and speak their minds, but their decision to make their point by "going on strike" and dancing to conga drums seemed to make light of a very serious issue. She had her military orders in hand; she would be leaving her home, her family, and her twin sister with no clear indication of how long she might be gone. She was shipping out. She had to drop her classes and to accomplish this she had to make her way through the crowd and get to the registrar's office.

The news story that was supposed to be about the peace rally became a news story about a brave, young, female soldier heading off to war. That night she told the reporter, and southeast Wisconsin, that she had received her orders, and though it would be hard to leave her family, especially her twin sister, she was going to answer the call.

"I'm ready to step up and do what's asked of me for my country," she said.

The announcer finished, "Now, with her death, many are saying her family has sacrificed enough."

I had been so engrossed in the lead-in video segment, I was a little disoriented when it ended; it was like someone suddenly turned on the lights on in a dark room. Katie Couric started the interview, "John and Lori Witmer are the parents of the three sisters. Mr. and Mrs. Witmer, good morning and our deepest sympathies, we're so sorry for your loss."

Our responses were sluggish. Being emotionally and physically spent slowed our reflexes, and her words took just a little longer to register. This, combined with the satellite delay, created an unnatural lag in the exchange, giving the conversation a somber tone.

"Tell us about Michelle."

Lori responded that we would need the rest of the show to do that topic justice, to describe her sense of humor, her commitment, and the way she seemed to bring light wherever she went.

"Rachel and Charity: Do you know where they are now? Do you have any idea?"

"They're making their way back to Wisconsin; we expect to see them sometime, today."

Had we been thinking clearly, we would not have given out such specific information. That statement would come back to haunt us later that morning.

"What have these months been like for you and your husband and the rest of your family?"

"It's been difficult."

"When your daughters joined the National Guard, did you ever imagine that they would be deployed and serving for more than a year in Iraq?"

Now I found myself admitting, on national television, that I was clueless, "No, I had been out of touch with this and my daughters did a good job of only giving me enough information to keep me happy; a few years ago when my daughters started talking about going places like Sarajevo and El Salvador, I was stunned. I didn't know that's what was done. So, it's been quite and adjustment. I never thought we would have daughters in situations like this. I always thought they would be somewhere, here in the States, maybe doing something in a support role, and it's been quite a shock."

"Have they said that they'd like to stay in Iraq and continue doing their jobs? Did they say, Lori that they wanted to come home? Have they expressed any kind of feelings about this to you?"

I began squirming in my chair. She was asking us, point-blank, if our daughters were onboard with what we were doing. Lori sighed deeply and answered, paraphrasing what Rachel told us the night before, "I know that they're very conflicted. They have two families. They are trained and committed and loyal and give a hundred percent to their work. They're very conflicted."

I jumped in and stammered out, "We talked to them for the first time last night, and we realize that although we were expressing our family's grief in the fact that it would seem unbearable to see them go back, they had to bring a different perspective on it. They're so concerned that we not violate the chain of command—that we understand they have a commitment to all those people that they have been serving with—and this is a real dilemma, because we need them home, but they feel committed to serve, and what we're trying to do is work through the chain of command, here, to try to find an arrangement that will work and allow them to complete their service. But again, in the end, Katie, they're going to make the decision."

Lori added, "Of course they want to come home; but they are also very committed to their jobs and their comrades who would lay down their lives for one another. This is a deep conflict." And now the world was privy to the "deep conflict." Public fascination with the conflict would continue for weeks to come, changing our lives forever.

"And how are you all feeling about the situation in Iraq? Obviously the violence has escalated considerably; do you feel like the United States is right in being there, fighting this war?"

It was like a sucker punch. Our daughter had been killed less than three days earlier, we were tired and grief-stricken, we were worried sick about our surviving daughters, and now we were suppose to intelligently answer a question about whether the U.S. should have been in Iraq in the first place. Does losing a child in a war suddenly make you an expert on international politics? I could only guess about the motive behind the question, but it seemed designed to draw and emotional response, one that would make good television.

I paused, I sighed, and then I felt energy rising up inside me. The words came pouring out in rapid succession; it was like I was listening to someone else speak.

"Katie, let me tell you what Michelle told me. We talked about this in great detail, and we know this is a very difficult issue and politically it's very hard to sort out, but she *knew* she made a difference and she knew that she made a difference in the lives of everyday Iraqi people—*especially the women*. She was so happy to know that women were now coming out on the streets—that they were now looking her in the eye. She felt that she had made a difference in that culture and that there was a liberation that went on. She was also very concerned that if we had a knee-jerk reaction to some of these horrible things that are happening, that thousands of Iraqi people would suffer from a swift exit. I don't know what the answer is, but she knew that it wasn't going to be easy and she knew that we needed to make sure that we did what was right for the majority of the Iraqi people."

Joni was watching from the adjoining room. She said she could see it come over me. She said it was Michelle, that Michelle was giving me the words. Joni's like that. I don't know if I can accept her explanation, but I've never been able to completely discount it.

"Well, Lori and John Witmer, I know you must be so proud of all your girls and again, our deepest condolences. You'll be in our thoughts and prayers as you get through this."

"And we're clear," one of the techs said as the video monitors' screens went to test patterns. They helped us take off the microphones. We collected ourselves for a moment and moved into the hallway.

Jim, the producer who had arranged the interview, buttonholed us: "We'd like you to stay a few more minutes and do a segment on . . ." He began rattling off the names of cable news shows and their anchors, none of which registered. Lori and I both shook our heads. He continued to list interview opportunities. We continued to shake our heads. We were done. We had given the one interview we had promised and we were done. It still took us a few minutes to get that point across.

Chapter 14 - Directive 1315.7

After the *Today Show* interview our home phone became useless. We had a listed number and by the time we got home, the call volume was so heavy we couldn't make outgoing calls; every time we picked up the phone, there was someone on the phone, calling in. Our voicemail box had a twenty-message limit and the messages came in faster than we could clear them. We stopped answering the phone, leaving it to Joni and other family friends.

I hadn't considered the ramification of mentioning, on national television, that Rachel and Charity were coming home later that morning. Now we were getting calls from friends advising that they were seeing news reports from the airport. Camera crews were waiting for our daughters' flight. The last thing we needed was to reunite in public. As we talked through this, Joni went to work, fishing out a card that had been handed to her when a Waukesha County Sheriff's Deputy came to our door, offering both his condolences and any assistance the department could render.

Until then, I had never really understood the connection between the civilian police and the military police. They explained that Michelle's death was the death of a fellow police officer and they would be there for us. The New Berlin Police force did the same, sending extra patrols by our house and checking in often.

Joni pointed out that we were in no condition to drive ourselves to the airport or to face the crowd we would draw once we were there. She called the number on the card and spoke to the Deputy, explaining the situation and asking for help. Not only did they send a van to take us to the airport, they worked with the Milwaukee County Sheriff's Department to have us taken directly to the airport tarmac. We waited for our girls on the tarmac by the stairs that led to the jet way. The Sheriff's Department got a message to the pilot, and the flight crew arranged for the girls to deplane first. They came down the steps and in a private space created by the baggage carts and tow motors, we held each other and cried. The duffel bags were delivered to the van and we made our way out of the secure area.

Rachel and Charity had barely seated themselves before the words came spilling out of them. "She had such a peace about her these last few weeks; it was if she knew," Rachel said, as she leaned in and lowered her voice, trying to keep the conversation in the family.

"She was ready to go," Charity continued, in the fluid way our daughters always engaged in conversation; rapid-fire, quick exchanges, finishing each others' sentences. They talked about her changed demeanor, about her rededication to her faith but most of all the peace she seemed to possess. I listened carefully to their words, but I wondered how much it was being interpreted through the lens of grief. It was both comforting and puzzling. The implication was that Michelle had been prepared for her death, that she had a premonition. I would come back to this thought over and over again in the months that followed.

As we arrived home, Rachel and Charity stared wide-eyed at the collection of satellite trucks, news vans, and reporters camped in front of our house. The van dropped us at the back door and the police presence seemed to keep the reporters at bay. We had been home only a few minutes when General Albert Wilkening, Adjutant General of the Wisconsin National Guard, came to our door. Rachel and Charity immediately assumed a military bearing, standing at attention, every sentence ending with a "Sir." The General tried to put them at ease several times, but they found it difficult to comply. He sat with us in our living room and addressed Rachel and Charity. He told them if they wanted to be reassigned stateside, he would see that they were reassigned. If they want to go back to Iraq, they could go back. If they wanted out of the Guard all together, he could make that happen.

I was stunned. I had hoped that the girls would have options, but I sat, speechless, as I tried to comprehend what he was saying, tried to understand this complete reversal. I didn't understand how things could have changed so quickly, but I was so relieved I didn't care. I began chattering, trying to persuade my girls to grab this offer before it vanished as quickly as it had appeared. I told them I didn't think I could hold it together if they went back. "You need to be with your family," I told them. I just wanted this part of the nightmare to be over. But Rachel and Charity politely asked me to leave the room.

They spoke to the General at length, and when the conversation was over, they repeated what they had said the night before: "It's not time to make a decision; it's time to focus on laying Michelle to rest. Can you give us time to make a decision?" The General assured us he could give them they time they needed.

From that point on, the Wisconsin National Guard was by our side, helping us navigate every step of the way. In the weeks that followed, the staff that was sent to support us became like family, and the bonds that were formed during that time have endured.

It would be years before we understood what had transpired behind the scenes. I am told that General Denson, the man I had lambasted on the phone, was indeed correct when he said that Army regulation made no provision for reassignment. But several people at Wisconsin National Guard headquarters had worked through the holiday weekend researching the question of compassionate reassignment, and they discovered a Department of Defense directive that trumped Army regulations:

DOD Directive 1315.7 Military Personnel Assignments

5.11.1.1 If a Service member of a family is killed or dies when serving in a designated hostile-fire area, other Service members of the same family shall be exempt on request from serving in designated hostile-fire areas or if serving in such an area shall be reassigned from there.

The directive was clear: "on request" surviving family members can be exempt from serving in the same hostile fire area. So why didn't the General know this?

When the National Guard is deployed overseas, they become part of the Army chain of command. The decision about our daughters' reassignments was out of General Denson's hands. This also meant the Governor, who normally acts as the Commander-in-Chief of the Wisconsin National Guard had no authority in this situation.

As the reference number suggests, there are thousands of pages of directives. A "directive" is not a law, and Army directives are updated whenever it is deemed necessary. DOD Directive 1315.7 – "Military Personnel Assignments," was updated in January 2005 when it was reduced from a 67-page document to three pages. The section about reassigning family members out of hostile fire areas when another family member is killed in action is gone, along with large sections dealing with the exemption from hostile-fire areas for sole-surviving sons or daughters. Apparently the slimmed down all-volunteer military, with its heavy reliance on reserve forces, can no longer afford the compassion it once had for soldiers and their families.

The flowers began arriving Monday morning, trucks doubling up in the driveway; drivers coming to our door in a steady stream. Now the sunroom's white tile floor was covered with baskets and planters and pots of every shape and size, and they overflowed from the table and the window sills. There were dozens of them, most of them from people we didn't know, all building to form a floral shrine. Tuesday morning the mail carrier showed up with stacks of cards, hundreds of them, some with only fragments of an address like, "The Witmer Family, New Berlin, Wisconsin." They poured in all week long; at one point there were so many they were delivered in a big bags. Eventually the gifts and letters would overwhelm the sunroom and spill into the living room, where many of them would remain for the better part of the year. Lori would insist that the tubs of letters, pictures, plaques, CDs, banners, quilts, flags, and display cases be left in the living room. She insisted that they would not be removed until we had reviewed each one and properly thanked those who sent gifts. Even after the thank-you notes had been sent, she couldn't bear the idea of packing it all up. The letters, cards, and gifts reminded her of how much people cared and she drew strength from them.

It's difficult to describe what it's like to see your own house, live, on the evening news. The reporters' vigil outside our home continued. Our pleas had fanned the flame of public interest, and now it was overwhelming us. Our efforts shifted to finding a way to step out of the spotlight. Joni began to develop a strategy. She reasoned that if the family held a press conference, there would be less of a reason for reporters to hang around the house. She also reasoned that if the news conference were held somewhere besides our front lawn, the herd of reporters would move from our street corner to the news conference site, and with luck, they would feel no need to return to our neighborhood. She worked with the Wisconsin National Guard to set up a press conference.

We began working on a second statement. Elmbrook Church had offered to let us hold the press conference at their building, a large complex in Brookfield, Wisconsin, with multiple auditoriums and meeting rooms. On Monday afternoon, we passed out flyers, explaining that the family would be holding a press conference the next day. By Tuesday morning, the crowd outside our house had thinned considerably.

It was a good plan, but we would learn that we had underestimated public interest in the story. We truly believed the spotlight would fade once we laid out the facts: that Rachel and Charity had the option to accept reassignment and that they simply wanted time to consider their decision. In our statement, we asked for some privacy so we could turn our attention to laying Michelle to rest.

But it was not to be.

4 ÇARŞAMBA 14 Nisan 2004 — Takvim

'Kızlarımı verin'

Irak'ta görev yapan 3 asker kızından 1'ini kaybeden Amerikalı aile, diğer kızlarının eve dönmesini istedi. Son kararı, Pentagon verecek!

Vitmerlar, Irak'taki kızlarından 1 yıl daha ayrı kalmaya tahammül edemeyeceklerini açıkladı.

Asker kızlarını Irak'a gönderen Amerikalı Vitmerlar, çok pişman. Bağdat'ta hafta sonu kurulan pusuda 20 yaşındaki kızları Michelle Vitmer'i kaybeden John ve Lori Vitmer, onların için Wisconsin'e gelecek kızlarının artık Irak'ta göreve yapmamaları için ABD ordusu nezdinde girişimde bulundu.

'AYRILIĞA DAYANAMIYORUZ'

"Bir yıl daha böyle yaşayamam. Ben ve ailem, buna dayanamayız" diyen John Vitmer, Wisconsin Ulusal Muhafız Komutanları'nın bu taleplerini Amerikan Savunma Bakanlığı'na (Pentagon) iletme ektini verdiğini belirtti. Ailenin yakınları da, diğer asker kızlarının Irak'a göreve gönderilmemesi için, Wisconsin'in senatörlerinden yardım istedi. Vitmer ailesinin Irak'ta görevli 2 kızının, çarşamba günü yapılacak cenaze töreninden önce evlerinde dinmaları beklenşiyor. Anne Lori ise, ağlayarak, kızlarından 1 gün daha ayrı kalmak istemediğini söyledi.

ERKEK ÇOCUKLAR, ASKER DEĞİL

Irak'ta hayatını kaybeden Michelle'in 32. Askeri İnzibat Birliği'nde bendasıyla aynı görevde bulunan 34 yaşındaki abları Michelle'in görev süresi, uzatılmıştı. Michelle'in tek yumurta ikizi Charity Vitmer'i de geçen yıl Wisconsin Ulusal Muhafız Birliği'nden, Irak'taki 118. Sıhhiye Taburu'na gönderilmişti. Vitmerlar'ın, 3 de erkek çocuğu bulunuyor. Ancak, onlar asker değil...

(Soldan sağa) Michael, Michelle, Lori ve Charity ... Vitmerlar, Michelle'in cenaze töreni için bir araya gelecek.

REAL MADRID ...

'Sosyete ...
ben geliy...

Kral ile

YILDIZ TİLBE

Chapter 15 - Angels of Mercy

The notion that we could somehow reach closure sooner if we could get the funeral behind us shaped our decisions in the days that followed Michelle's death. We were uncertain when her body would be returned to us, and this created a dilemma: waiting to have the memorial service until the body was returned could have meant waiting over a week before we gathered with friends and family, and we couldn't wait that long. We needed the support of our loved ones; waiting a week seemed like waiting forever. We decided to hold a memorial service the Wednesday following Michelle's death and then conduct a private burial when the body was returned.

Who makes plans to lose a child? Who thinks about burial plots and church services and all the planning that goes into a funeral? We were completely lost. Michelle had not left a will; there were no written instructions about funeral arrangements. My sister stepped in and recommended a well-respected funeral home, and now we sat in our living room talking through the arrangements with the funeral director.

The first question was "Where?" I had regularly attended Elmbrook Church in the years preceding Michelle's death, but I was not a member. The church is attended by thousands of people on any given weekend, and I was only involved on the periphery. My friend Joe Glatzel intervened. He picked up the phone and called the Elmbrook church office, and explained the situation. He was put in touch with Pastor Scott Arbeiter who immediately reached out to our family, explaining that the church would be there to support us and that the facilities would be available to us.

In the week that followed Michelle's death, Joe was there for us, over and over again. He would show up at odd hours, in the middle of the day when he should have been at work. He planned all the music for the memorial service and offered to direct the musicians. Joe ended up taking the entire week off work, a fact I learned only when I pressed him in the weeks that followed.

Pastor Scott, from Elmbrook Church was equally amazing in his dedication to serving our family during the weeks, months, and years that followed Michelle's death. He spent hours with us that week, trying to help the family work through what had become a second crisis: a strong disagreement on how to honor Michelle's last wishes. Charity firmly believed that Michelle would not, under any circumstances, want her body viewed, by anyone, including her parents. Lori had last seen Michelle four months earlier, and she desperately wanted to see her daughter one last time. It was a mother's love versus a twin's dedication to her twin—two of the most powerful forces on Earth were colliding. They wrestled with this decision for hours in what would often become a heated exchange, with Pastor Scott doing his best to mediate.

I had been sent to pick up supplies for the picture boards that Sara, one of Michelle's best friends, was assembling for the memorial service. On the way, I realized it had been quite some time since I had eaten. I wasn't really hungry but I needed a break from the planning, I needed to sit at a counter, wearing a baseball cap, blending in with the retirees and the delivery drivers and lose myself in a bowl of soup. I needed just ten minutes to do something normal.

"Normal" didn't last long. After I finished my soup and got into my car, I turned the key and the radio sprang to life. The unmistakable voice of one of Milwaukee's drive-time talk show hosts surrounded me. He was dialoging with a caller, "… I just don't think it's right."

"Why should they get special treatment? They signed up to do a job and they should do it," the caller chimed in.

The host said, "We're talking about the father in New Berlin, who went to the *media,*" he spat out the word "media" with disgust, " asking for his daughters to be reassigned! I don't think the daughters are asking for reassignment, it's the *father!*"

He barked out the station's call letters and continued, moving to the next caller, "I agree with you," the callers almost always did, "he shouldn't have gotten the media involved."

The host droned on every afternoon about the sins of "liberals and lefties" with a shtick that, from my perspective, was bigotry dressed up as political analysis. For the most part, his callers lined up to agree with and adore him for being the voice of political conservatism in Southeast Wisconsin. I shouldn't have listened. The last thing I needed was to have this dialogue rattling around in my head, but the drive from the restaurant was less than a mile, which meant I only had a couple minutes of exposure to being the target-of-the-day on Milwaukee's angry-old-white-guy show.

We had a driving need to make the memorial service something that would have a lasting impact on all who attended. The service was our opportunity to tell the community who Michelle was, why we loved her, and why her life and death had meaning. It had to be well planned, it had to be perfect. We poured all our energy into putting together a service that was worthy of Michelle.

The elements of the service came together in ways that left us marveling. Michelle had spent time at her friend Sara's house when she was home on leave in December. Sara's mother called to pass along the title of a song called "Legacy" by Nichole Nordeman. She said Michelle had listened to the song when she was visiting, and made a point of saying how much she liked the song and its message.

I sat at my computer after downloading the song and cried as I listened to it; it was if Michelle were speaking through the words, like she had sent us this message:

I want to leave a legacy,
how will they remember me?
Did I choose to love? Did I point to You enough
to make a mark on things?

I want to leave an offering,
a child of mercy and grace who
blessed your name unapologetically,
and leave that kind of legacy.

I knew instantly that this would be the song we used in her memorial video. I had no idea how I would find the time to scan and sequence all the pictures we had selected, but I was determined it would be done and done well. By the night before the service, I hadn't managed to scan my first picture. I was planning on staying up all night if necessary to get this done. But Elmbrook's director of video services just showed up at our front door. I had met him only once, in passing, and that was months earlier. I don't know how he knew I needed help, but he took the stack of pictures out of my hands and the CD with the song and told me not to worry about it, that it would be ready for the service.

93

Amidst the planning, we continued to fine tune our statement and our plan for the Tuesday-morning press conference. It was agreed that Joni would read the statement and that we would not take questions. We would exit the room after the statement was read, leaving the Wisconsin National Guard's public relations officer, Tim Donovan, to talk to the media.

On Tuesday morning, Rachel, Charity and I left for the press conference, early, because we had to stop at a copy shop to have handouts made. As we drove toward Brookfield, Rachel asked, "Do you mind if I smoke?" Rachel—health-conscious, athletic Rachel was asking if she could smoke in my car.

"Sure," I said, not bothering to ask when she'd started smoking.

"Rachel, pass one back to me," Charity said from the back seat.

A few years earlier, I would have gone through the roof if I had ever caught them smoking, and even as adults I would have, under normal circumstances, read them the riot act. But now it seemed insignificant. Life was short, they were in pain, and if smoking a cigarette would make them feel better, the least I could do was let them smoke it in peace.

After meeting briefly with Pastor Scott, we filed into the room to a blinding eruption of camera flashes. Dozens of cameras, all set in rapid-fire mode, produced a wave of clicks that seem to go on forever. Joni was introduced; she would be reading the statement. The intention was to keep the event dignified and grieving parents, reading a statement with wavering, halting voices, would not serve that goal.

April 13th Statement

We would like to extend our profound gratitude for the outpouring of support we have received from both home and abroad. We would also like to express our deepest sympathy to those families who have lost loved ones in service of their country.

Rachel and Charity would like to express to their fellow soldiers in the 32nd MP Company and Company B 118th Medical Battalion: "Our thoughts and prayers are with you. Not a minute goes by that we don't think of you. We are conflicted, because we have two families and we can't be with both at the same time."

Yesterday we received news from Lieutenant Colonel Tim Donovan of the Wisconsin Army and Air National Guard, who is with us today, that Charity and Rachel will not be required to return to Iraq. According to Defense Department Directive number 1315.7, service members who lose a family member in hostile action can be exempted from service in the hostile action at their request.

At this time, Charity and Rachel are deferring their decision regarding their future plans. They are focusing their attention on spending time with their family and grieving the loss of Michelle.

A public memorial service for Michelle will be held at Elmbrook Church, tomorrow at 7:00 p.m. A private burial will take place at a later time.

In response to requests, the Michelle Witmer Memorial Fund has been established. Contributions will benefit the Missionaries of Charity Orphanage in Baghdad whose ministry to handicapped children made such a profound impression upon Michelle.

In hindsight, our family's appearance at the press conference did not serve us well. We had reasoned that if we did not appear at the press conference, some reporters might remain camped out in front of our house. Announcing the public appearance had the desired affect; an hour before the press conference, all the reporters and news vans were gone. That much went according to plan. What we hadn't thought through was the image we presented: six of us, holding on to each other, a large family grieving the loss of their soldier-daughter and sister. This heartbreaking image would appear on the front pages of newspapers around the world.

After the news conference, there was a tidal wave of new inquiries. We were contacted by hundreds of media organizations from around the globe: England, France, Australia, Israel, the list went on and on. Every major network sent producers to our door. And for reasons I never really understood, Hollywood gossip shows pressed us for interviews. We sequestered ourselves as best we could in our New Berlin home and waited for the storm to break.

אחיות
לצרה

שלוש בנות נידלו ג'ין ולורי וויטמאר
בפסטורליה אמריקנית. התאומות מישל
וצ'ריטי והאחות הגדולה רייצ'ל התגייסו
למשמר הלאומי כדי למימן לימודים. הן
לא חלמו למצוא את עצמן בלב המאפליה
של בגדד. באפריל חזרו השלוש הביתה.
מישל שבה בתוך ארון. משפחה שהיתה
החלום האמריקני בהתגלמותו, מנסה
עכשיו לחבר את השברים

גדעון קצן, וויסקונסין
מילים ומני ניישראי o

Chapter 16 - Sleepwalking

I realized the beauty of the business model as we stood in the warehouse chain store that specialized in men's suits and promised to make alterations in twenty-four hours or less. I had suits, but they were dated; with the advent of "business casual," there had been no need to buy new ones. Tim had outgrown the suit we bought for him when he was sixteen. I had outgrown mine by adding twenty pounds during the previous year's vigil. Now we both needed suits and we needed them quickly.

"No, I don't have anything in mind—something dark … "

"Yes, I do need shoes."

"A dress shirt? Sure."

"Yes, the tie looks nice, I'll take it." They led us around the store and we accepted whatever they handed us. Given our state of mind, they could have sold us the clothing racks and the store fixtures.

"Tomorrow—we need them tailored by tomorrow. We have a funeral to go to."

Seven hundred dollars later we left with a claim check and a bag full of accessories.

The two hours of visitation we scheduled before the service was not enough to greet even half the people who had lined up in a stream that extended out the door of the large sanctuary, through the visitor's center, and beyond. Friends, neighbors, veterans groups, soldiers, and total strangers, hundreds of them, waited patiently to express their condolences. We were advised to take frequent breaks to guard against fatigue, but we felt compelled to receive as many people as we could; we never left the front of the sanctuary. About a half-hour before the service was scheduled to begin, Pastor Scott explained that Governor Doyle had asked to see the family, privately.

We were ushered into a small meeting room where the Governor, after expressing his condolences, addressed Charity and Rachel directly: "I want you to know, that if it were in my power, I would order you to take reassignment." He said our family had given enough and now it was their duty to support their parents and help their family

97

grieve. The room was silent as Rachel and Charity considered the words of the man who in normal times was the Commander-in-Chief of the Wisconsin National Guard. In the end, they did not offer an answer, and the Governor did not press them for one.

Most of the dignitaries made their appearance at the visitation, gave their sound bites to the press, and left. Governor Doyle stayed and spoke at the service and then, rather than exiting into the wings and leaving through the side door, he returned to his seat and remained through the entire service. His care and concern for our family seemed genuine. Later that year, he would begin the tradition of inviting Wisconsin's Gold Star families, families who had lost soldiers, to the Governors' residence for a holiday reception, a low-key event with no press, just a way of showing that the State of Wisconsin and its Governor remembered the sacrifices our families had made.

We left the meeting with the Governor and followed our guide to a room behind the auditorium, one normally used for choir practice. With fifteen minutes before the service began, we straightened ties, sipped water, and composed ourselves. When it was time, we reentered the auditorium through a door beside the platform.

I was unprepared for what I saw and felt in that moment. It was mystical, what some would describe as a burning-bush experience. As we walked out, we could see the large auditorium filled with hundreds and hundreds of people, care and concern radiating from their faces, reflecting the presence of God with an intensity that is difficult to put in to words. It was one of those moments in life where the separation between the material and spiritual becomes thin, when it is easy to believe, easy to feel the presence of God.

In the year preceding Michelle's death, I had struggled with my faith. The daily anxiety generated by having daughters in a war zone had worn me down. During this time, God seemed aloof, distant, and uninvolved in my life or the affairs of this world. After seeing an interview on the news of a mother who had lost a son in the war, telling viewers that her faith would see her through, I remember connecting the dots in my mind. This woman, this good, Christian woman, had lost her son in Iraq. Her prayers for protection had not been answered, so what made me think my prayers would be answered? What made me think that I had a special deal with God, a guarantee that my daughters would return to me safe and whole. This woman's story shook me to my core, and I began questioning everything I thought I believed.

As I stood looking out over the congregation, "confusion" did not begin to describe my mental state. I was comforted and angry at the same time. In the last twelve months, I had desperately needed to *feel* God, and yet I had felt nothing. Now, in this moment, in this place, I felt God's presence, but it both comforted me and angered me. It was as if God decided to show up at my daughter's funeral instead of preventing it. I would spend years trying to make sense of this.

A cascade of candles surrounded by roses stood before the large portrait of Michelle, in green camouflage, wearing the official army beret, her name displayed above her pocket, a smile gracing her face. Joe Glatzel, dressed in a dark suit, sat at the grand piano, leading the musicians as the honor guard moved to the front of the auditorium with precise movements and choreographed steps. Joe's face betrayed his heavy heart as his hands moved across the keyboard with the grace and precision that only years of performing can bring. The stars and stripes lay across a wooden pedestal in the front of the auditorium in the spot a casket might have been. The stage was flanked by large, poster-size portraits of Michelle, one picture of her smiling in her tan, desert uniform and one, slightly more formal picture of Michelle in all her glory, in civilian dress, with full make-up, styled hair, and sporting a fur collar.

Dignitaries assembled in the front row; Governor Doyle; General Wilkening, the Adjutant General of the Wisconsin National Guard and other Wisconsin National Guard top brass. The honor guard placed the colors, and after an opening hymn, General Denson began his remarks, "This is a sad day for the Witmer family, the Wisconsin National Guard, and the United States Army as we say goodbye to a daughter, a sister, and a fellow soldier."

I wanted to be respectful of General Denson, but it was difficult. This was the man who came to tell me my daughter had been killed. This was the man who told me that Army regulations dictated that Charity and Rachel were required to return to the same hostile fire zone that took their sister's life. His face was the one I associated with all the pain we had been through and, fair or not, I was angry with him.

It would be over a year before I was able to put myself in his shoes. He was a General; he could have sent someone else, but he personally took on the difficult assignment of notifying us of Michelle's death. I didn't want to hear what he had to say, that Army regulations required my daughters to return to their units, but it was true, and it would have been much worse if he had promised something he had no power to deliver.

Why didn't he know about the Defense Department directive allowing for reassignment under the circumstances? The reason was simple; it had never come up. It had been decades since the Wisconsin National Guard had to deal with a combat fatality, so how could they be experts on the ever-changing regulations that govern such events?

General Denson continued, "The following message was forwarded to the Witmer Family by Sergeant Nate Olson, who was in the Humvee with Specialist Witmer when she was killed, and I quote,

While driving, we heard small arms fire, nothing unusual, followed by a loud explosion. I looked at everyone in the vehicle at that time, and everyone appeared fine. It was nothing new. This has happened before. We usually just drove out of the kill zone to safety. But this time, it was different. After the explosion, an RPG, rocket-propelled grenade, was fired at our middle vehicle and heavy gun-fire ensued. It was coming from everywhere, ground-level, second-story windows, roofs, etc. Most of the gunfire was directed at our vehicle. This was a well-planned ambush, and their intention was to render our middle vehicle inoperable, causing us to stop. Michelle was hit as she attempted to engage the targets. She did everything right. Unfortunately, the gunfire was too heavy, and concentrated on our vehicle. The lieutenant and I rendered first aid to her in the vehicle.

She is a hero. And it was my honor to serve with her. She will never be forgotten. Because of her quick reactions, she undoubtedly is the reason why I am here today.

Thank you Michelle.

Signed, Sergeant Nate Olson, 32nd MP Company, friend of Michelle.

I would think about Olson's statement for months, trying to understand the events of that night. The description of the circumstances of the ambush left me unclear as to how Michelle's actions saved his life. For months, I imagined Michelle laying down covering fire, allowing the convoy to drive out of the kill zone. But then I realized it was much simpler than that; she saved his life because she was *there*, because *she* was in the turret. Someone had to be there. Someone had to be the most exposed member of the crew. The simple act of taking her turn in the turret that night meant someone else got to go home.

Governor Doyle took the podium. "To the Witmer family: the state of Wisconsin has lost one of its finest daughters, Michelle Witmer," he went on to deliver a brief but stirring tribute. Charity wept openly as he concluded his remarks, "Michelle makes us proud to be from Wisconsin, she makes as proud to be Americans."

Next, Colonel Mark Bruns took the podium and read the citations that accompanied three medals being presented to Michelle, posthumously. We had met Colonel Bruns when he showed up at our door with Lt. Julie Garity the Monday after Michelle was killed. I didn't know what to expect from either of them. Colonel Bruns handled public relations and Major Garity was the Causality Officer for the WNG, and although I didn't remember it, she had been one of the officers who came to our door on April 9. Garity and Bruns would be constantly at our side for the next several weeks, and our admiration and respect for these two officers grew each day they were with us. In the months and years that followed, they became part of our family.

General Wilkening presented the medals to the family, as Col. Bruns read the citations, and with each medal, the General dropped to one knee and spoke quietly as he placed the medal in our hands, "On behalf of a grateful nation … " The care and compassion General Wilkening displayed made a deep impression on me.

Somehow we found the strength to take the platform. Many advised us against speaking at our daughter's memorial service. They pointed out that the risk of standing up and then not being able to speak was very real. They pointed out that it was one more burden we were picking up at a time when we already had more than we could bear. But as Lori would go on to say, we wanted the whole world to know how much we loved "our Michelle."

It was agreed that the best way for the audience to gain insight into who Michelle was would be to read some of the things she had written. I began with this letter:

October 11, 2003

Dear Everyone,

As always it's wonderful to hear from all of you, and I apologize for not writing you back individually. I really wish I had the time. I just wanted to give a quick update on my life.

Well, Baghdad has cooled down quite a bit and it feels a lot like summer in Wisconsin. There have been rumors about it getting as cold as 65 degrees, and I'm holding tightly to that dream. Right now I am working the night shift, patrolling and doing force protection at an Iraqi Police station. Pretty much the same kind of work I've been doing the last few months. Saturday is my only day off a week, and it's not really a day off so much as time to catch up on your duties. It usually consists of doing laundry, cleaning your weapons, vehicle and personal area, and then seeing if you're needed for anything else and after that you get to relax. I look forward to it all week, so when I was told this past Saturday I would have to pull duty for the commander I was pretty disappointed.

I was tasked out to be on escort duty with about five other people. We ended up escorting him to an orphanage run by nuns. It reminded me of everything I'd ever seen in a movie about an orphanage in a third-world country. The surroundings were very plain; it was basically a few rooms with cribs side-by-side. The children were between the ages of six months and ten and all of them were handicapped in some way. One of the Sisters explained to me that when a child is handicapped or ill, it's not uncommon for them to be left for dead in Iraq. We came to visit with the children for about an hour and it moved me to see how much just holding a child or saying kind words could affect them. They were so joyful and happy to see us.

The sisters were so amazing; most of them were from India but there was one from Italy, they all spoke English, and it was wonderful talking with them. One, in particular, just sat and talked with me for awhile. She told me she'd been in Iraq for three years and before that in Lebanon, and other countries. Her whole life was dedicated to working with orphaned, handicapped children. A life of service, even though Iraq, a predominantly Muslim country, isn't very welcoming to Catholic nuns. They had nothing but positive things to say, they were some of the kindest women I have ever met, it made me want to weep seeing some of these children, and I can't imagine how difficult their job must be at times.

Being a Christian here, denominations and interpretations melt away and it just becomes as simple as God loves us, so we can rejoice. It was when I was holding one of these children that I realized I have so much to be thankful for.

Love,

Michelle

She was thankful. She was eight thousand miles from home, in a place that she told us smelled like garbage, a place where she risked her life every time she left her camp. She had been pulled away on her one day off, and in the end, she found something to be thankful for. This was her gift, taking the lemons life handed out and making lemonade.

Lori took the podium and, for a few, very tense moments, it seemed as though we should have listened to those who told us not to do this. I silently prayed she could get the words out. And then she began to read her favorite e-mail from Michelle, one of the last she had written, only days before she was killed. The subject was simply "Daddy."

Tuesday, March 30, 2004

Hey Dad,

It was a warm night in Baghdad there was a slight breeze in the air and the dark clouds above looked as though they were toying with the idea of opening up and releasing their fury on the dimly lit city below. The young woman running on the path that paralleled the Tigris River was secretly praying that they would open and cool her perspiring forehead. She panted along as she took in the beauty of scenery around the river to her left and across from it the city lights. To her right were the ruins of what were once some of the most magnificent palaces in the world. It would only be a few weeks before this chapter of her life would be over. A year ago, a student in college whose only concerns were making rent and restocking the Ramen noodles, Michelle could never have dreamed how in one year her life had turned into a top that couldn't seem to stop spinning. It had spun her all the way to

Baghdad, Iraq and turned the course of her life upside down.

As she neared the home stretch, she pondered how this year had changed her perspective on life, culture, war and things worth dying for. She began to think about her many experiences, some would call them adventures, some nightmares, but she preferred to think of them as spices that gave the story of her life richer flavors and saucier smells. Yes, her life had definitely gone from TV-dinner to world-cuisine. "Maybe someday I'll write a book about all this, give it my own personal spin," she thought to herself as she began her cool down.

Okay pops, maybe I will write a book about this place someday; who knows. Let's see, I went running tonight and thought about how much I miss you guys. Well I miss you and love you and I will try to be better at writing more!

Love your daughter,

Michelle

Lori yielded the podium to Charity, who started with a story about a conversation she and Rachel had with Michelle when they were little. They were all sitting around talking about what they wanted to be when they grew up. Rachel wanted to be an actress or a singer; Charity wanted to be a marine biologist.

"Keep in mind, we were ten years old," Charity continued, "and Michelle just looked around and said, 'You know what, you guys, I really want to be a hero.' Rachel and I look at each other and said, '*Sure*, okay' and Michelle says, 'No, seriously, I *think* about it. Maybe I could push someone off of a bridge and then jump in and save them and then I could be a hero.'"

All around the auditorium, smiles pushed their way through tears as Charity continued, "This was Michelle; I mean *this was* Michelle."

The audience broke into to laughter as Charity explained that Michelle often failed at her attempts to be rebellious, like the time, when she was fifteen when she and a friend stole a six-pack of beer for a night of revelry only to learn the next day that they had stolen nonalcoholic beer. They laughed again when Charity described Michelle, in the third-grade, letting her best friend, Sara, cut her bangs right before picture day with the choppy results being captured for posterity.

"Michelle loved *this*," Charity continued, motioning toward the crowed. "She loved the drama; she loved 'the cheese.' She *loved* telling stories. She *hated* when I told stories."

> When I would tell a story, she would say, 'Come on, get to the point, come on!' because I like to take my time. And today, when I decided I would come up here, I could just hear her saying 'Charity, you better not make me suffer by going on and on and on.'

Charity slowed as she continued, "And I felt her today— her strength. And I know she's with us."

Charity's words flowed with grace and poise until she said, "One of the last times I saw Michelle," the words caught and her lips pressed together, betraying her sadness, "she gave me a big hug and a kiss and she said, 'I love you.' And that was such a gift from God. I want you all to know that Michelle was at peace and in *such* a good place when she left this world."

Rachel and Lori, who flanked Charity during her talk, instinctively reached for her as her voice began to quaver, placing their hands on her shoulders. Charity continued to address the audience, determined to say the words she felt were so important. "I didn't understand why she had to go. When they came and told me what had happened, I said, 'Why? Why? *Why, God*, did she have to be the only one that died that day!? Why was it her?'" Rachel's face reflected the pain that crossed Charity's face as she struggled to continue.

And the chaplain, who Michelle had come to know very well, in the two weeks before her death, said 'Charity, I feel like God laid it on my heart to tell you, because she was the only one ready to go.' And she was. She was ready and she was at peace. It is so important that you all know that. Michelle had had a hard year. She had seen things that *nobody* in this world should have to see. She had seen the worst of Iraq, and yet she kept her faith in God and in humanity and in her mission and was the best soldier that she could be. And she *was* a hero when she died. It wasn't because she saved someone from a lake, but she was a hero when she died. And she was at peace. She's in a better place now.

When she was young, Michelle, displaying her typical independence, attended youth services at another church, the one her best friend, Sara, attended. That's where she met Pastor Brian. Pastor Brian was one of those people who seemed to be sure of his calling, sure that he was supposed to shepherd young people. Michelle had always been drawn to genuine people, and Pastor Brian was the "real deal," and she told us so on several occasions.

Life had taken Michelle and Pastor Brian in different directions. Pastor Brian had moved on to a church in Dayton, Ohio, but when we lost Michelle, we could think of no one better suited to eulogize her. He presented a message titled, "The Gospel According to Michelle," and like every good sermon it had three main points: start trusting God wherever you are; lead with your heart; and follow God, even when you don't understand him.

"I don't know if you could stay in a room with Michelle for more than twenty minutes that she would not give maximum effort to put a smile on your face. She was energy in motion," Pastor Brian said.

Then he did something none of us expected. He nodded to the sound technician and Michelle's voice filled the auditorium. She was addressing some students at a youth retreat, telling them about some tough times she had recently been through, telling them to keep on believing and to keep on trusting God and that He would see them through. Hearing her voice, hearing these words at the service for the first time, was a gift, one of many we would receive that night. People all over the audience reacted emotionally to her words; some cried and some smiled. Later I would marvel that Michelle had given part of her own eulogy.

Pastor Scott came to the platform as he explained the closing ceremony. He said that Michelle had shared the light of God's love with those around her and we, too, should take that light into the world in memory of Michelle. Lori and I lit our candle from the candle in front of Michelle's picture, and our surviving children lit their candles from ours, and then our extended family lit their candles from our children's. I watched as the candlelight spread through the auditorium as the musicians sang the song "Go Light Your World."

Another wave of wonder and awe swept over me as I watch a visual representation of the way Michelle had touched so many lives as the small flames fanned out across the entire auditorium, until the entire assembly was bathed in candlelight. The congregation spontaneously rose to their feet for the last verse of the song. We followed the Honor Guard out of the auditorium, as the song was reprised, and with that procession we marched into a life without Michelle.

On Thursday morning, we received notification that Michelle's body would arrive in Milwaukee on Thursday evening. This was much sooner that we had expected, but we spent all day Thursday making arrangements for the burial. Now we called relatives who had just left town and let them know the burial would be held on Friday, "No pressure, we said, "we just thought you should know that we will be laying her to rest tomorrow." But as we said it, we knew we were putting them all in a difficult spot.

The family gathered at the airport cargo hanger late on Thursday evening. The sun had nearly slipped below the horizon, and only a small red ember glowed in the western sky. The Honor Guard was there for the transfer of the casket to the hearse. Pastor Scott met us at the hanger, and after the Honor Guard completed its task, he pulled us together in a circle and prayed with us; prayed *over* us really, asking God to help us through the coming days. As a pastor, he knew better than any of us what lay ahead, that we were only beginning our journey into grief, and this was reflected in the earnestness of his prayer.

Thursday night was quiet—too quiet. All of the out-of-town family had left, Rachel and Charity had gone to Tim's apartment, Mark was with friends. I felt as empty as the house.

Chapter 17 - Casualties of War

The two worst moments of my life were separated by seven days, bookends on what seemed like the week from hell. The knock came on April 9th, 2004; we laid Michelle to rest seven days later on Friday, April 16th.

It was one of the most beautiful spring days I'd ever seen, standing out like a shining jewel from the parade of gray and chilly days that had preceded it. As the funeral procession moved through the city, every intersection was sealed off to allow us to travel, unencumbered, from the funeral home to Wood National Cemetery, a military cemetery in Milwaukee. I doubt that a presidential motorcade would have received better treatment. The police departments of all the communities along the way worked in concert to make this happen. At every intersection, after the cross traffic had been stopped; the officers turned and saluted the procession, honoring our Michelle.

Wood National Cemetery was green and beautifully manicured with huge, majestic trees standing over rows and rows of white headstones, all standing at attention, all standing in formation. The wooden casket, with its gold handles, sat on a pedestal in front of rows of chairs. The flag had just been removed and presented to Lori and now it was time to say goodbye.

Our children went first. And that's when it happened, the second worst moment of my life—the moment I watched my children approach their sister's casket. You could see the pain cut through them like a knife. I had lost a daughter to war, but it was then I realized that my surviving children were being maimed by that same war, sustaining injuries that would follow them for the rest of their lives, wounds so deep it made me wondered if they would ever be able to function again.

Rachel wore a simple black dress, one that would be appropriate for any formal event. Her hair was pulled back, revealing the slender lines of her face. Through the whole ordeal, she had been stoic. There had been moments of reserved tears, but for the most part, she had played the part of the good soldier. Now, as she approached the casket, the grief surged out of her. The image of Rachel, with her forehead on the casket, her body racked with sobs, will never leave me. At that moment, I feared for her; at that moment, I realized how wounded she was.

Mark gently stroked the casket as he slowly lost control. He knelt before the casket and he, too, wept openly. It had been hard for him because he was only sixteen when his sisters had marched off to war. His relationship with Michelle had not matured; she often treated him like the annoying little brother. Part of him had still been angry with Michelle for the way she needled him about being "the baby" or "mom's favorite," for the way she always tried to correct him and boss him around. She had never really known him as the man he had become, and now she never would.

Charity never attempted to hide her grief and rage. Her sister, her twin sister, had been taken from her, and if she could have found the man who shot her, I have no doubt she would have made sure he died a slow and painful death; made sure he suffered as much as she did. She was angry and hurt and she made no apologies for the way she felt. It was an honest anger, a powerful anger. She, too, placed her hands on the casket and stood over it while the grief poured out.

Tim's wounding had started long before that day at Wood National Cemetery. It started when the war took his sisters across the ocean. From an early age, Tim had been labeled "gifted." He leapfrogged through school, skipping grades and graduating early. He had a semester of college courses under his belt long before his eighteenth birthday. He had backpacked across Europe before he turned twenty. But when his sisters were sent off to war, this bright, confident young man folded. He sat in his apartment watching war coverage on the cable news shows for hours. Like all of us, he was looking for any sign that it would be over soon.

When it became apparent that the Iraqis had not received the Americans as liberators and that our soldiers were facing a protracted, guerilla war, when it became clear that his sisters would be spending the next year overseas, this young man, this smart capable young man who never ceased to amaze bosses and teachers alike, just shut down. He stopped going to classes; he didn't even bother to withdraw. He stopped answering his phone. When he finally pulled out of the initial depression, he still had trouble doing anything that made him face the reality of the situation—that his sisters were staring death in the face every day. He simply carried on as if it wasn't happening. It was his way of coping. Now Michelle was gone, and it tore at him. She was gone, and he had barely written to her. He covered his face, as if to hide one more time from the harsh reality of war.

Lori sat beside me holding the carefully folded flag, maintaining her composure but obviously fighting to do so as she took in, for the last time, the wooden coffin in front of us, a coffin that was never opened for her. Charity said Michelle had made it clear that should she die, she would not want a viewing, that she would want to be remembered as she was. It was one thing to talk about death in the abstract, when we all thought it would be decades away. But now Michelle had been cut down at twenty years old, half a world away. How do you tell a mother that there will be no last look, no final goodbye?

Pastor Scott sat with us for hours as we wrestled with this decision, talking with us together and apart, trying to find some middle ground. He suggested a viewing only for the immediate family. Charity was adamant, defending what she felt were Michelle's last wishes: "If you open that casket I'll never speak to you again!" Lori had already lost one daughter. The price of seeing Michelle one last time seemed to be losing another.

"We don't have to tell Charity," I suggested. We can slip out for an hour, go to the funeral home, and say goodbye." Lori dressed to go to the funeral home, but she never left her room. She couldn't do it. "I can't risk losing Charity, too," she told me. I desperately wanted to find a solution, but in the end, I could do nothing.

I barely remember getting out of the folding wooden chair. I barely remember standing in front of Michelle's casket or getting back in the car. I think that's why I went back to the grave so often. I hadn't seemed real. I had trouble believing it had really happened.

Years later, while transferring files from an old computer, I found this e-mail Charity sent to Tony, the man who would become increasingly more important in her life, the evening of the day we buried Michelle.

Tony,

I am writing this through tears, because it just hurts! WHY??? WHY THE F--k DID IT HAVE TO BE HER???? I am so sad—so unbelievably devastated. I hate waking up and remembering she's not there. I HATE IT TONY!! I just want to crumble—to sink. I just see her casket, and having to say goodbye; my parents both were inconsolable. Today was the worst and I just can't breathe; I can't sleep because I hate waking up and having those five seconds when you don't remember what happened then have to realize all over she is really gone, my sister, my twin, my best friend. My heart is just aching; I feel so broken.

Tony I don't know what to do; I don't know if I should go back or stay. Do they need me? It would kill my dad . . . it would just kill him and my brothers if I left. Tim sobbed, begged me not to go. What do I do? I am so lost.

~ *Charity*

Chapter 18 - The Crush of the Crowd

It was months later when my little sister, Anna, finally called me on the carpet. It hadn't really registered while it was happening, but the crush of attention created a barrier around us, one our extended family could not penetrate. Michelle's aunts and uncles and grandparents were also grieving her loss, and during the time when families normally come together to support each other, Lori and I were mounting a campaign to have Rachel and Charity reassigned.

A family pleading for the reassignment of their surviving soldier-daughters added another dimension to an all ready heart-wrenching story. The storm of public attention became a raging river, sweeping us along, always downstream from our family. They were forced to watch, from a distance, as we mourned the loss of our daughter.

I have eight brothers and sisters. Lori's parents are still with us and she has three siblings. When we lost Michelle, they dropped everything and came to be with us. They came to sit with us, to cry with us, to have quiet conversations of consolation and remembrance. But these moments never happened. They sat on the couch while we jumped up every few minutes to deal with some urgent matter. Someone from Washington is on the phone. There's a call from Iraq. Someone from the Senator's office wants to talk to you. There's a police officer at the door wanting to know if he should clear the street in front of the house. It went on and on. And it always ended the same way, "We can see you're really busy; we'll come back when things quiet down."

But things didn't quiet down. Not for a long time, anyway, and by then the damage was done. We had lost the opportunity to support each other in those critical days that followed Michelle's death. There's no knowing how differently things would have turned out had we chosen to stand by, passively, and simply hope that things would turn out well for Rachel and Charity. We'll never know if it was worth what it cost us; if it was the right decision; if we could have gotten the same results without adding fuel to an already raging media fire.

At the time I write this, there are still some family members who are estranged as a direct result of the events that followed Michelle's death, adding broken relationships to the toll Michelle's death took on our family.

To say the family was in the spotlight would have been only partially correct. It wasn't just one spotlight; it was several, shining from different angles. Each facet of the story amplified the public attention; each element interacted with the others in a geometric progression.

First there was the fact that Southeast Wisconsin had been following the story of the three Witmer sisters going off to war for over a year. When we lost Michelle, many in our community, who had followed the story in the newspapers or on television, felt the loss with us. Then there was the fact that Michelle was the first *female* National Guard member, to be killed in action, the first ever. Not just in Wisconsin, in the entire nation. She was the first *Wisconsin* National Guard fatality since World War II. This underscored both the changing role of women in war, and the changing role of the reservist, and this would serve to fuel debate over the military's policy in both these arenas.

The changing role of reservist was highlighted by the length of the deployment of the citizen-soldiers of the 32nd MPs: fourteen months. At that time, it was one of the longest deployments in recent decades, but it seems modest when compared to the mind-boggling twenty-two-month deployment of a National Guard unit in neighboring Minnesota. These were part-time, weekend warriors, doing fourteen-month tours while their regular army counterparts rotated in and out in six months.

These elements alone would have likely propelled the story into the national spotlight. But when we took up the campaign to have our daughters reassigned, the story went around the world. People sent us magazines and newspapers from France, Turkey, and Australia. We received e-mails and letters from England, Germany, and Iraq and those are just the countries I remember. We received hundreds of request for interviews, many from foreign journalists, and our daughters' faces were on the front pages of Turkish newspapers and other Middle-Eastern publications.

Our daughters were offered the option of reassignment less than twenty-four hours after the Sunday afternoon press conference; we had what we wanted, and we had neither the need nor the energy to continue making public statements. But we quickly learned that if you don't talk to the press, the press will to talk to anyone with the slightest relevance to the story. Our extended family began to get calls. We saw our neighbors, some we barely knew, on TV, answering questions about us. One reporter even interviewed a waitress at the diner we frequented.

The misinformation began to spread. We received a call from a family member of a soldier serving with the 32nd MPs. One of our relatives had given an interview, and it was now being reported that, during their time in Baghdad, Michelle and Charity were not permitted to spend time together. This came as quite a surprise to the leadership of both the 32nd MPs and the Company B 118th, who had gone out of their way to provide such an opportunity, arranging for Charity to be transported to Mustang Base from BIAP so she could spend a day off with Michelle and Rachel only two weeks before Michelle was killed. In hindsight, it was an extraordinary gift to our daughters. Now it was being reported in the news that the girls never had such an opportunity, leaving all those involved in making it happen feeling unappreciated.

"The Witmer Family Website", a website I created to provide our extended family with the most current news about our soldiers, was mentioned in many of the stories and articles. Shortly after we lost Michelle, the website, "hit" counter spun up from five thousand to half a million. People from all over the world used the comments section of the website to send messages to the family. Most were condolences, like the message we received from an individual identifying himself as an Iraqi Kurd, thanking us for Michelle's sacrifice and proclaiming "the Kurdish people will remember her as a martyr." But some were disturbing, like the one that had the subject line "One less War Mongering Witmer;" it suggested that Rachel and Charity would be next. There was no way to know if this was from a crackpot or from someone with ties to the insurgency, but it underscored the fact that the Witmer sisters' faces were known around the world.

By the Monday following Michelle's death, we were being overwhelmed by flowers. Setting up a memorial fund seemed to be the right thing to do, and Lori, remembering Michelle's letter, felt strongly that she would want us to direct this outpouring of compassion to the orphanage. Our former neighbor and longtime friend Judi worked at a local bank and she offered to setup the Michelle Witmer Memorial Fund, and we made reference to the fund in our last statement to the press. It was just one more element of the story that captured the public's imagination. A series of stories about the orphanage and the memorial fund appeared in local newspapers and on local television, and donations poured in.

As the next few weeks unfolded, I tried to give Rachel and Charity the space they needed to make their decision, but I couldn't leave it alone. I was frustrated that the Army's position was that Rachel and Charity had to *request* reassignment. I felt it should have been automatic under the circumstances. How do you expect a soldier who's lost a sibling to return to combat and not be handicapped by the experience?

I wanted the decision taken out of Charity and Rachel's hands and I had no reservations about working behind the scenes to see if I could make that happened. I had received a call from Tommy Thompson, former governor of Wisconsin, who was serving as U.S. Secretary of Health and Human Services. He offered his condolences and said if there was anything he could do for us, "just ask." It dawned on me that I should take him up on his offer—call him and ask if he had any friends at the Pentagon. It was then I realized that he hadn't left any contact information. I was so desperate I looked up the general number for the United States Department of Health and Human Services and waded through the recordings hoping to find a way to reach Thompson. After twenty minutes on hold waiting for an operator, I realized I was grasping at straws.

We waited for public interest to wane. The girls were granted a fifteen-day extension to their emergency leave in hopes that the longer they waited, the less interest there would be.

But in the end, the extensive news coverage drove our daughters' decision. On April 27, there was one last press conference announcing their decision. The Adjutant General's statement read, in part:

If I could make the decisions for Charity and Rachel, I would make them.

If I had the power to order them to complete their service outside of Iraq, I would do that.

But I do not have that power, so yesterday afternoon I told them, using all of the influence I have, that they should complete their active duty military obligations outside of Iraq.

My direct request to them was based not only on the needs of two soldiers and their grieving family, it was also based on military considerations for their units and the safety of 225 other Wisconsin Guard soldiers whose exposure to danger might well be increased due to the international visibility these units received over the past two weeks.

Rachel and Charity abided by the General's recommendation and accepted reassignment.

I had done what I set out to do, but at a tremendous cost. The day Rachel traded her desert BDU for a green uniform was one of the hardest days of her life. She called me the first day she was to report for duty at her new assignment with the Air National Guard and said she didn't know if she could put on the uniform, the green uniform that meant she wasn't going back to join her platoon, that meant she wasn't going back to Iraq. But she did put on the green uniform and reported for her new assignment: guard duty at the Milwaukee airbase. She pushed through the mundane days and weeks and took comfort in the fact that it would only be for a short time, just until the 32nd MPs came home.

Charity was reassigned to the unit's headquarters in Waukesha, doing paperwork. In less than a week she was so bored she was climbing the walls. She pushed to be transferred to MEPS, the Military Entrance Processing Station, in Milwaukee, where at least she could use her medical training. "I need *real* work, not make-work, work that will make the days go by quickly," She said.

After the press conference announcing the decision, we continued to receive dozens of request to make public appearances: parades, conferences, and rallies. These invitations presented a dilemma. We wanted to honor Michelle's memory, we wanted people to remember her, but each event was like a mini-funeral, physically exhausting, emotionally draining. We limited ourselves to government and military events, trying to avoid anything with political overtones, feeling that this is what Michelle would have wanted us to do.

In May, the Wisconsin State Senate issued a proclamation honoring families of the fallen, and they asked us to attend. A few weeks later the State House issued a similar proclamation and we were asked, once more, to attend. We couldn't do it. It was too hard.

Chapter 19 - The 32nd Returns

On July 22, the 32nd MPs came home and we were asked to be present at the homecoming. We made the two-hour drive north to Volk Field, where the plane carrying the returning soldiers would touch down. I watched the tearful reunions and thought about what it would have been like to see Michelle come off that plane. To grab her and laugh and cry all at the same time, to sit with her in the makeshift reception area with the other families, savoring every minute of the few hours we had together before our soldiers would be loaded up in buses and taken back to Fort McCoy for the last few days of out-processing.

Several soldiers eventually made their way over to us, expressing their condolences and then talking to us about Michelle and sharing stories. The men who had been with Michelle the night she died approached us with solemnity and respect and told us about her last few moments. They wanted us to know that she wasn't in pain, that her death was nearly instantaneous. They explained how they attempted to revive her, how even after they should have known it was hopeless, they kept trying, taking her to the field hospital, hoping, against all odds, that something could be done. She couldn't have been in better hands. Both of the men who were with her were medically trained. I got the sense that this was more than a courtesy, that these men truly cared about my daughter and that her loss had moved them deeply. Years later I would read that one of them still carried Michelle's picture in his wallet.

Another soldier shared a story about how Michelle used to feed stray dogs that came around the compound, remarking that at one point, a litter of half-wild pups were following her around. He was dumbfounded and laughed with us when I explained that we now had one of those "half-wild" pups.

It was said of my mother, Gail Witmer, "that she never let a baby go un-kissed or a dog go un-petted." In that respect, Michelle was very much like her grandmother. Tripod, a dog with one bum leg, began hanging around the compound that Michelle and the rest of the 32nd MPs called home. Others tried to chase the dog away, but when Tripod had a litter of puppies, Michelle couldn't help herself. She fell in love with them. She took a special liking to one female pup she named Charlotte. The dogs must have been born sometime in early February

2004, because the puppies appear to be about six-weeks old when Rachel, Charity, and Michelle had their pictures taken with them the day they spent together in Baghdad in mid-March.

Michelle did not give us even the slightest hint that she was involved in a plot to bring the dogs stateside, and she made no mention of the fact that *she* was planning to adopt one. A week after Michelle was killed, a sergeant who served with Michelle called to tell us of the arrangement. And on May 5, 2004, Charlotte arrived in Wisconsin. The sergeant's wife met us in the Walgreen's parking lot to make the handoff—the last in a long line of transfers necessary to bring these dogs halfway round the world.

Charlotte was a big fur ball. She looked like a collie pup with the color patches slightly askew. Her muzzle and ears were black, her body was camel colored, and she had white-tipped paws on three out of four legs. She smelled bad after a two-day trip in a wood crate, so after thanking the sergeant's wife we went directly home and gave her a bath. We quickly discovered that she was all hair.

She loved the grass in the front yard and was soon frolicking with Charity on the lawn. When Charlotte got tired, she would simply fall over, lying on her side until she got the energy for another run. We took the dog to Tim and Rachel's flat, and then Charity and Tim took Charlotte for a walk, disappearing for a long time. Rachel and I finally figured out that they had walked to Wood National Cemetery. They wanted Charlotte to be able to pay her final respects to her patron, Saint Michelle, rescuer of needy animals.

Charity was determined to train Charlotte and train her well. She read up on house training puppies and tethered Charlotte to herself when she was in the house. Charlotte however, constantly wanted to let people know she was submissive, and in canine fashion, she demonstrated this by urinating every time someone came into the room. The official term for it was "submissive urination." This was not a mild case; the dog made a puddle at the drop of the hat. She also defied conventional wisdom by soiling her crate on a regular basis. It became clear that it would take a great deal of time and effort to deal with this behavior. But this was Michelle's dog, and we romanticized about how Charlotte would become a part of our family, a bundle of love, helping us to mend. We decided to keep her outside until we could come up with a better strategy.

We had a small, unfenced yard, and we put Charlotte on a long chain. She immediately demonstrated her superior digging abilities, excavating deep holes all over the lawn. It took us several months to admit we couldn't handle Charlotte. We contacted the sergeant and let him know we needed to put the dog up for adoption. Like an answer to a prayer, one of the sergeant's coworkers expressed interested in Charlotte. She had a big, fenced yard and a several other dogs and cats. At least Charlotte would get her happily ever after.

Rachel joined the soldiers boarding the bus for Fort McCoy. She would rejoin her unit for the five days of demobilization, and our family, like all the other families, was asked to return to Fort McCoy later in the week, for a "family briefing." At the briefing, counselors explained to the soldiers' families that there would be a period of readjustment, and that patience would be required as their soldier re-entered civilian life. But getting soldiers and their families, who've been separated for fourteen months, to sit still and pay attention, was nearly impossible.

Chapter 20 - The Spotlight Fades

I sat on the black leather couch in the TV room, holding the large, rectangular remote control for the ancient VCR in my hands, scanning the tape, trying to find the spot where the interview began. It was Wednesday, September 8. We had gotten a call from the producer telling us the interview would run today. I had to be at work, so Lori recorded it for me. But I worked only a few miles away from our house, so I came home at lunchtime to watch the tape. I fast-forwarded until I saw Michelle's picture on the screen and then backed up the tape a few seconds. Diane Sawyer, co-anchor of *Good Morning America,* was finishing an interview with Madeleine Albright and she began her transition:

> Every life is a treasure but emblematic of each of them, perhaps, is this woman: Twenty-year-old Army Reserve Specialist Michelle Witmer. She and her sisters, all three of them, were serving in Iraq when Michelle died in an ambush. And we spoke to Michelle's sisters, Charity and Rachel, in an exclusive interview and they told us about the pain that they feel every time they hear another name go on that list.

The interview had been recorded a few weeks earlier in anticipation of a grim milestone: one thousand combat fatalities in Iraq and Afghanistan. Michelle's picture fills the screen as the lead-in video continues; she is dressed in her desert BDUs and poses in front of a building somewhere near Camp Victory in Iraq.

A stately hotel room fills the screen as the interview begins to roll. In the frame, Diane Sawyer is seated on the left facing Rachel and Charity on the right; they are connected by a band of sunlight pouring through the windows in the background. Fresh flowers are centered between them adding color, standing out against the somber colored wardrobe all three are wearing.

"When you hear of another death in Iraq does it just make the day that much harder all over again?"

Rachel answers, "It's like getting punched, pretty much every time you hear about it." It is the first time she's spoken on camera since

Michelle's death nearly four months earlier. She and her sister were barraged with requests for interviews from every kind of television and radio show. Oddly enough, some of the most persistent requests came from entertainment shows that focused on celebrity gossip.

Charity continues, "You'll hear it on the news, 'two soldiers were killed today in Baghdad.' It's a two-second news blip. We just want to cry because we know the pain—that's *somebody*. Somebody people love and care about and they just lost them; it's just *two seconds* on the news—it's just hard." She says this through tears, and the tone of her voice conveys the pain she feels as the screen returns to a live shot of Diane Sawyer as she explains that the full interview will be coming up later in the broadcast. The show moves on to world news as Charlie Gibson continues " ... Russia, of course, is in mourning after last week's terrorist attack that left over three hundred people dead, many of them children ... "

I watch the bottom of the screen where the time is displayed, and I advance the tape until it reads 7:30. The interview leads off the second half-hour of *Good Morning America*. "So here are Michelle Witmer's sisters, Rachel and Charity, talking about the war and the cost of love and grief."

The lead-in, composed of family pictures and videos, rolls as Sawyer's voice sets up the story: *"A family scrapbook, five children, three of them girls, arm and arm, soul to soul since they were born. So much laughter, mischief, love; and of course when one enlisted they all did."* The viewer sees clips of all three sisters from their last Christmas together and then the news coverage of Michelle's burial as the voice-over continues, *" Just one beloved life of the one thousand lost."*

The video fades as the interview returns to the screen. "Tell me about Michelle as a soldier."

"She was *so* dedicated to her job," Rachel volunteers and Charity finishes her thought.

"She was great with people."

Charity explains that Michelle used to give the street kids candy and toys, "She *loved* kids."

The screen fills with more pictures of Michelle as Sawyer's voice-over describes her for the viewers, *"Michelle, the good, the insecure, the seeker."*

As Rachel talks about Michelle's last few days, the camera takes a close-up of her as the graphic; "Sisters in Arms" appears at the bottom of the screen. "She came to me the day before this happened, and she sat me down and she said 'I just need to talk to you.' She started to tell me that she knew that everything is going to be okay. She said, 'I don't know what it is, but I'm okay; I'm at peace with everything.' She said *those* words, 'I'm at peace with everything.' She said, 'I'm not worried about what's going to happen when I get home anymore. I'm not worried about what my future holds; I'm not worried about what goes on here. I know that God has a plan for me; I know he will take care of me. And I am okay.'"

Sawyer describes the events of Michelle's last night on earth as pictures of Michelle in body armor appear on screen; one catches her as she sits in the gunner turret of her Humvee, talking on the radio. Charity returns to the screen as she tells the story of receiving Michelle's last e-mail, just a couple of hours before she left for her last mission, and she breaks down again as she remembers Michelle's last words to her: "I just want you to know I love you forever."

"You saw her that day?" Sawyer asks Rachel.

"When we left that day, we lined up in vehicle convoys, and she was going to one part of the city and I was going to another. I was in a gunner turret and remember looking over and seeing my sister in a gunner turret and thinking, '*That's odd, she's usually the driver.*'"

"So I kind of smiled at her and she smiled back and I remember,— and I will kick myself for the rest of my life—having this urge to just run over and hug her and tell her 'I love you to be safe.' And I didn't. I also remember the look on her face. It was more stoic than usual and she just—I don't know if people know what's going to happen to them—but she had this calm, stoic look on her face, and I waved to her and she kind of smiled at me and waved back, and that was the last time I saw her."

Charity adds, "She just was *so* at peace with herself and with life, and in retrospect it's just incredible to me. It was like she *knew*."

Charity repeats the story she told at the memorial service about her conversation with the chaplain the night Michelle died. How she had asked him why it had to be Michelle, and how he replied that he felt God wanted him to tell Charity that it was because Michelle was ready to go.

Sawyer's voice-over continues as she recounts how Michelle died in an ambush as scenes from the memorial service and the burial pass by. "*A nation was riveted on their bond, their loss, and the choice facing the two girls left behind. Rachel and Charity say everything inside them wanted to go back with their other family, their military family the ones still in harm's way."*

Back to Rachel as she says, "I'm just supposed to walk away from that and be okay with staying home and knowing that my family, in a sense, is still overseas in this horrible conflict? On the other hand, how do I look in my parents' faces who have just lost a daughter and tell them, 'I'm sorry, but this is my duty, I have to go back?'"

Sawyer voice explains, *"In the end the military was worried that publicity had made them targets and advised the sisters to remain at home."*

Back to the hotel room as Sawyer continues, "Do you think there should there be a rule that families can't send more than one child?"

"No," Charity responds without hesitation.

"You don't?" Sawyer challenges, her tone reflecting amazement.

"No," Rachel reiterates.

"That's not asking parents to bear *too much*?" Sawyer presses.

Charity responds by explaining that if, at eighteen, you can be trusted to vote and make contracts then, "you have to make your own decisions."

I shared Sawyer's amazement at their response. I wanted rebuttal time. I felt strongly that if the military placed no restrictions on family members serving together in combat, then they should at least have a policy that made reassignment to non-combat duties automatic when a family member is killed in action. It wasn't just siblings serving side-by-side; in this war, there were fathers serving with sons and husbands serving with wives. The all-volunteer, reservist-heavy military had made these situations relatively common.

Sawyer addresses Rachel, "Do you go to the grave site?"

"It's hard. Every time I think I'm strong enough to go and talk to her—because that's what I want to do when I go—I don't get more than a couple words out before I'm an absolute mess. It always overwhelms me because it's always full of flowers and ones my family didn't put there; there's always flowers. It's just overwhelming to see how many people's she's touched."

Sawyer continues, "When you hear people talking now about the war in Iraq and what's going on in Iraq, do you want to stop each and every one of them and say …"

Charity jumps in, "You know, it's just such a complex issue, and I think my biggest problem with people, when they state their opinions about Iraq, is they make it so black and white. And it couldn't be further from black and white."

"And at the same time," Rachel adds, "when these people give us these opinions, good and bad, Charity and I have both talked about the fact that there's really not much people can say to us that will hurt us anymore. Because that's their opinion, the very opinion that we have the freedom to have in America and voice, the very opinion that Michelle was willing to give her life for."

Brief clips from local news broadcasts around the country roll by, each featuring a newscaster reading about the death of another soldier. "When you hear of another death in Iraq, does it just make the day that much harder all over again?"

It's the portion of the interview that ran earlier in the broadcast, but this time Rachel's answer is longer, unedited. "It's like getting punched, pretty much every time you hear about it. Because not only do we know the circumstances that most of them were under when they died, but we know what the family is about to go through."

Charity's painful response is reprised and finishes the interview, "You'll hear it on the news, 'Two soldiers were killed today in Baghdad.' It's a two-second news blip. We just want to cry because we know the pain—that's *somebody*. Somebody people love and care about and they've just lost them—it's just *two seconds* on the news—it's just hard."

Diane Sawyer concludes the segment, live, back at the news desk, "And as we said, nine hundred and ninety-nine other stories like theirs."

Although there would be follow-up interviews from time-to-time, the Diane Sawyer interview was the period at the end of the media-coverage sentence. We had one more major event to get through, but this one would be different. It began with a phone call from a filmmaker. I was at work when I took the call. He had called the house first and Lori had given him my work phone number. She would have only done this if she felt there was a good reason for me to talk to him. He explained that he was producing a documentary for HBO. It would be called *Last Letters Home* and it would feature families of soldiers who had been killed in action, reading letters from their loved ones. He had read some of the letters from Michelle, on our family website, and he asked if we would consider being part of the documentary. It had only been two months since we lost Michelle when he called, and we knew that working on the project would be difficult, but we felt strongly that this would be a fitting tribute to Michelle. She wanted to write, she wanted to be a journalist, and having her letters be part of a documentary seemed to be a way for her writing to be shared with possibly millions of people.

A few weeks later camera crews converged on our house and set up in our back yard. Lori, Charity, and I sat in lawn chairs and read three of Michelle's letters for the cameras and talked about Michelle and our family's loss. A still photographer came by a few weeks after that to take pictures of the family, the letters, and some of our keepsakes. These would later become part of the film's companion book.

The film was to air on Veterans Day 2004, but HBO arranged for a screening in Milwaukee, in late October, renting the vintage Oriental theater and asking us to provide the names of up to four hundred people so that they could be invited to the Milwaukee Premiere of *Last Letters Home*. The theater was full. Our family and friends were in attendance, and many of Michelle's friends from the 32nd MPs turned out for the showing. When we saw the film and the book that accompanied it, there was no doubt in our minds that it had been worth the pain.

Chapter 21 - Picking up the Pieces

In the days after we lost Michelle, I would get up every morning at 5:00 a.m. and start drinking coffee; it was the only thing that kept me going, and I needed a full hour and several cups before I could find the courage to face the day. As I drank my coffee, I would read. I read dozens of books in the months following Michelle's death, trying to find some wisdom and trying to make sense out of what happened.

I began to realize and accept the fact that I was angry and that, for the most part, I was angry with God. My entire adult life, I had taken my faith seriously. I attended church, I gave regularly, I brought my children up in the faith; I worked hard and sacrificed to send them to Christian schools. Yet for all my dedication, God had still allowed my daughter to die in an ambush. I felt God had let me down and I was angry and I boldly told my pastor this when I met with him. I expected to be chastised for being sacrilegious; instead, to my surprise, he simply told me it was okay to be angry, that it was okay to question: "God is big enough to deal with your anger and doubt. Keep talking to Him; be honest. More than anything else, that's what God wants from you."

I bought a journal because I need a place to keep track of the books I wanted to read, and on the first few pages, I wrote: *The Light Beyond; Life at Death: A Scientific Investigation; Plato: The Myth of the True*; *Recollections of Death: A Medical Investigation; Surprised by Joy; The Great Divorce; Man's Search for Meaning.* As I read the books, I took notes, and from time to time, something I'd read would trigger a flow of words: angry rants, emotional thoughts, and theological musings. I would capture them in my little gray, leather-bound Wal-Mart journal. Writing seemed to ease the pain, at least a little. And the blank pages continued to challenge me to put my thoughts into words and then read them back to myself to see if they made any sense.

Journal Entry – July 2004

Black and White

I try to imagine who this man was, this man who killed my daughter. Did he believe that Americans are all godless infidels, intent on turning the Middle East in to Hollywood after stripping it of its oil?

Black-and-white thinking is easy. All it requires is sorting the things we encounter in life into two large piles, one labeled "good" and the other "evil." The man who shot my daughter had consigned her to the "evil" pile. He never met her, he knew nothing about her except that she was an American soldier, and in his black-and-white world, American soldiers should die. In the middle of the night, he and his comrades waited in ambush. From a window of a building, he fired on a twenty-year old girl from Wisconsin. *He* only saw her as part of an occupying army. *She* saw herself as a police women sent to protect the people of Baghdad from lawlessness. *She* sought to understand the strange culture she landed in. *He* understood only the slogans of hatred he had grown up with.

Did he lose a family member in the war? Was he a dispossessed follower of Sadaam, angry about being cast down to the bottom of the social hierarchy? Was he part of some extreme religious sect that sees all Americans as infidels and worthy only of death? What would have happened in his black-and-white mind if he had stopped, for only a moment, to consider that this soldier was part of a family, with a mom and a dad and sisters and brothers? Could he grasp that this woman was in his country as part of what she considered a call to duty, and a mission of service? Would it have mattered to him that this soldier respected the people of Iraq and their dedication to family and faith, their integrity and their will to go on.

I cannot hate this man. He suffers from the same problem many Americans suffer from; so willing to drop an entire people and an entire religious group on to the "evil" pile in their black-and-white world. When confronted with a culture they do not understand, they become bigoted, not wanting to spend the intellectual energy to sort it out. Hatred is so easy, so convenient, and it's so much easier to hate nameless, faceless people.

Journal Entry – August 2004

Landmines

If my brain is a small world inside my head, there are parts of this world that have not yet received the news that my daughter, Michelle, was killed in action four months ago. In these primitive parts of my brain, there is little communication with the outside world. As I wander through the weeks and months, certain events conspire to make a journey to these outposts necessary, and upon receiving the news, there is an outpouring of grief, brand-new grief. I never know when or what will trigger the awful news spreading to another part of my brain: a song, a person, an innocent question. The part of my brain-world that has lived with the news for four months no longer reacts to the pictures hanging on our living room wall or the medals and flags displayed on the mantle. Most of the time I can walk through this miniature-Michelle museum and not be affected by emotion; most of the time I can walk past her room unencumbered by feelings of sadness. Don't get me wrong, I am always aware of my loss—that low-level ache has become a part of my existence; I expect it to be there.

It was an odd phone call. I was at my desk, in my office, the same office I have occupied for eleven years, going about my daily routine. This routine allows me to escape into the mind-numbing hustle and bustle of the business world. The phone call was an unexpected and unwanted intrusion, a violation of the compartment I have created for myself in my work life, the place I go to pretend that everything is normal. My ability to get through the day depends on the compartment I have created, so this man on the phone, asking for Charity Witmer, is like a cold draft threatening my house of cards. *Charity Witmer? Why would someone be calling my work number asking for my daughter?*

"May I ask what this is regarding?" my voice already revealing my anxiety.

"This is Sergeant Smith with the Army property control department. I need to speak to Charity Witmer."

"How did you get this number?

"She listed it on her form as her work number"

"This is her father's work number. Who are you?" I ask again with rising irritation.

"Sergeant Smith with the Army . . .

I don't let him finish. I am performing a quick mental review of the emails I received warning of scams perpetrated on the families of fallen soldiers. Is this guy just fishing for information? Did he somehow get my work number as part of a scheme? Is he "working" me? Michelle's death and her sister's story were very high profile. Maybe this is a con man, trying to make a few bucks off a grieving family, like that movie *Paper Moon*.

"I'm sorry; I need some sort of verification." I am not aware of how loud my voice has suddenly become. I don't realize that everyone sitting near my office is now hearing this little drama. The voice on the other end of the phone gives me his number. I don't mention that it's the same number that is displayed on my caller ID, with an area code from some far-off place; I hang-up and call back immediately. The same voice answers the phone. This is not what I wanted. I wanted an official-sounding receptionist. Somehow this would have given the whole situation more credibility. But I have his phone number, so if he is scamming me, I can find him again.

"What exactly is it you want?" I ask at a volume still inappropriate for the office.

"Mr. Witmer, I have a box that is labeled for Charity Witmer, but in reviewing the contents we found a driver's license for a Rachel Witmer. We need to talk to Charity to sort this out." To me, his tone sounds like a detective conducting an investigation. He is not rude but not cordial either. He sounds like someone who deals with a lot of shady situations, like he's opened a lot of boxes containing stuff that shouldn't be there.

I use my I'll-talk-slowly-and-clearly-so-that-even-a-moron-can-understand voice. He doesn't deserve this, but I'm angry about having to say it, having to think about that dark night in that war-torn city when my girls were called into some drab, plywood Army field office and informed of their sister's death, ten thousand miles away from the family, who, at that exact moment, so desperately needed to hold them. "Rachel is Charity's sister. They were rushed out of Baghdad when their sister, Michelle, was killed in action so that they could escort her body home. Under the circumstances, I'm not surprised their things were mixed together. Just send the box to Charity. Rachel lives only a few miles away. We'll sort it out."

"Sir, I am sorry if this conversation has upset you," he says before hanging up.

Upset me? My throat has nearly closed. My eyes feel like they're being pushed out of my head. A coworker sticks his head in the door and says in a concerned voice, "Are you all right?" I am determined not to sit in my office with a window to the plant floor and cry in front of the whole world. I am angry that I am suddenly overcome by this situation. I wave him off with a mumbled response, and after he steps away, I pick up my keys and leave through the back door. I don't tell anyone I'm leaving. I just go. I get in my car and drive. I'm going nowhere in particular. And then I pull over because I can't see the road and the sobs are heaving out of me.

I am angry about not being able to find an isolated spot. I don't want people to see me. I recover enough to drive some more, but every square inch of the industrial park seems to be bustling with activity. "Damn it!" escapes my lips. I am not a swearing man, so this outburst surprises me. I just need to be alone, I keep driving, but I find no spot that looks safe enough to pull over and melt down. The last thing I want is someone coming up to my car and asking me, "Is everything okay?"

What other land mines await me? What other triggering events will cause me to travel into some remote region of my brain, bringing the horrible news that she is gone, causing yet another brain-country to declare a national day of mourning? I am finding that it's an awfully big world out there.

The summer following Michelle's death, Charity also began to journal, and she shared this entry with me where she describes the task of sorting through Michelle's things after large footlockers and a duffle bag were returned to us:

It's been over seven months, I think to myself as I stare at the duffle bag in my closet. I have been waiting for the right moment, the moment where I can summon the courage to open it again. I have been prepping all week for this moment, and I know what I have to do. I slowly walk over to my bedroom door and lock it. I need to be alone when I do this. I take a deep breath and pull the bag out of its hiding place. I find myself staring at Shelly's name and Social Security number, which are written on the side of the bag in black magic marker. I am already fighting tears, and began to wonder if I should continue. I find an open space and sit cross-legged on my bedroom floor, quickly emptying the entire contents of the bag in a circular motion around me, before I have the chance to change my mind.

I am overwhelmed with emotion as I look at the items surrounding me. I hold back a sob as I reach down and touch one of her shirts. I notice a plastic Ziploc with a letter from Jackson, her battle buddy who had packed the bag a day after Shelly died. She explained that she had done most of Shelly's laundry, but she couldn't bear to wash the shirts that still smelled like her, so she'd put them in plastic Ziploc bags along with Shelly's hairbrush. I opened one of the bags, and I understood what she meant as I inhaled the familiar scent of Shelly's J-lo perfume on one of her brown t-shirts. I began to sob, clutching it with a death grip, trying to hold on to all I had left of my twin sister, my Shelly. I didn't want to go on, and I don't know how long I sat there sobbing before I could gain any kind of control, but I knew I had to finish this. I knew this was something I had to do for her, knew she wouldn't want anyone else going through her personal things. It took every ounce of strength in my body to finish the task, and when I had finished, I knew another part of my soul had died, that day, and with that realization, the finality of it all.

The days are getting shorter and darker, and I am missing her more than ever. I miss her smile, and her laugh. I absolutely hate that I have to get used to the idea of going through this life without her by my side. I know I never will. I can only describe it this way: it feels as though my life is coated in this thick substance that makes every single common task, every movement, heavy and weighted. Most days I feel as though I have to work twice as hard to keep up with everyone else, and some days, like I'll never cut through it. In the meantime, all I can do is pray for strength.

Journal Entry – September 2004

Dear Michelle

I was driving home from work when it registered that it was fall; the leaves on the trees were brilliant hues of red, yellow, and orange. In years past, this would have simply been a passing thought. Now it was a "first": the first fall without Michelle. A wave of sadness came over me. When I arrived home, Lori was out, so I was alone with my grief. I saw my journal sitting on the table and I picked it up and began writing, the words flowing out as tears filled my eyes.

Dear Michelle,

It is the last day of summer. You died in spring. And spring turned to summer and now I am faced with fall and I miss you. I miss you more than I can say. It is so wrong that spring and summer have come and gone without you there to see them off.

I miss your laugh. It was your laugh, special, like a song every time you laughed it. I can hear it now, in my mind as I write this, and I want to promise myself that I will never forget it and that I will always be able to hear it in my head.

I miss our hugging ritual, a big bear hug and then squeezing each other until one of us begged for mercy.

I miss the way you could always sense what kind of mood I was in. You never had to ask what kind of day I had, you just knew.

You were always my cheerleader, always expressing wonder at the smallest of my accomplishments like they were a big deal. That's why people loved you so much. You always went out of your way to encourage people, especially if you thought they were feeling bad. It was your gift.

Last night I went to a meeting at City Hall. They want to name a park after you. All these wonderful people who want to help remember you have approached City Hall about renaming a park in your honor. I was so honored, but then it made me think about the fact that now you can only be remembered. No new memories. The ones we have will have to do for the rest of our lives, and that makes me so profoundly sad.

Your memorial fund has more money in it than we could have ever imagined, and as we work to get in into the hands of those precious nuns in Iraq, I am again reminded why we have the money, because people wanted to honor you, because you are not here, and it makes me cry.

I haven't cried this hard in a long time. Somehow today I feel your loss more heavily than I have in weeks. The changing of the seasons, the memorials, I'm not sure what it is, but it really hurts today. Maybe it's because of what your Mom asked me.

She asked me what we should do about Christmas. I told her I didn't want to think about it. We had planned to travel, get far away from anything that would remind of us what we have lost. Plan a grand distraction to try and ward off the pain of the holidays. The fact that it was close enough to talk about made me ache.

But Michelle, I need my ache, I need my pain, because I need to hold you close, I need the memory of you constantly with me because I can't bear to think about losing you, about letting go of you. I can't risk forgetting you no matter how much it hurts right now.

Love Always and Forever,

Dad

Journal Entry – *September 2004*

The Orchard

I am walking through an orchard and the apples are just right for picking. It is a beautiful fall morning in Door County, one of my favorite places on earth. It is difficult to describe the breathtaking beauty of the scenic vistas, like the one that looks out over Ellison Bay. As I wandered through the twenty-five-acre orchard I find myself doing something I had not been able to do in many months: I am praying.

My children would sometimes refer to Donna Teskie as "Auntie Donna." They met Donna through our dear friends, Fran and Neil Teskie. Fran is Donna's sister, and last Thursday, Donna passed away. She was barely forty-seven years old. She left behind a loving husband and five children, one not yet a year old. That morning her headache had become so severe the family called for an ambulance. A few hours later Donna was gone. A brain aneurism took her so quickly there was no time to even attempt the surgery that might have saved her.

Over the last ten years, our children spent summers working for the Teskies in their orchard and farmers' market. Lyle and Donna lived only a couple of miles from Neil and Fran, and their children worked alongside my children. They ran in packs during the summer months, and some of their fondest memories and wildest adventures happened during those summers in Door County.

When I arrived at the Teskies', the phone was ringing, people were at the door; family members were arriving from out of town. There were decisions to make, questions to answer, condolences to be received; it seemed like there was no end to the activity. Through the Teskies, I saw our family. I saw them dealing with the things Lori and I had to deal with when we lost Michelle six months ago. The family members were coping, their bodies were going through the motions, and their mouths were responding to questions, but their eyes had that look, that far-away look, a look that had pain and shock and grief all rolled into it.

I watched as those in the community came together to offer support. It was a heartwarming phenomenon. The acts of kindness were abundant: the food, the flowers, the dozens of ways people found to help the family. But there were also thoughtless acts. And, Dear Reader, I ask you to learn from what I am about to tell you. You need to understand that you can unintentionally inflict pain on the grieving, hurting them when they are least able to bear it.

First, if you have suffered a loss of your own, this is not the time to bring it up. If you do, you will be taking instead of giving, taking emotional support from those who can least afford to give it. Second, don't subject the grieving to uninvited theology lessons. "She's in a better place now" or "All things work together for good," are statements that may be true enough, but offered in this context only serve to minimize the loss of those grieving.

As I walked and prayed in the Teskies' orchard, I realized that I had given up being angry with God. His presence, that weekend was palpable. It was in the music the family had lovingly picked for the tribute. It flowed from the tender moments represented in the pictures and videos. It reflected in the acts of kindness the community had offered up to this grieving family. I could feel it; I could, once again, feel God's presence.

No, I don't understand Him, but I cannot deny his goodness. Yes, my theology is broken, but his love will help me pick up the pieces and give me comfort even when the answers are a mystery. I know there are many difficult days ahead, but somehow I feel ready to face them.

Chapter 22 – Sister Nirmala

October 2004

We knocked on the door of the plain, boxy, white building in a distressed neighborhood a mile or so from downtown Minneapolis. The nondescript building might have once housed a church or a day care center. I don't recall seeing a sign, but that didn't surprise me. It wasn't their style to have a sign. That's why it had taken six months to find them, this order of nuns who were like God's Special Forces. They moved quietly, behind the scenes, doing their work. Their stealth allowed them to go places inaccessible to other church and aid organizations. I learned that they often went into global hot spots when other aid organizations were pulling out because it had become too dangerous to stay.

Setting up the memorial fund for the Baghdad orphanage had been simple; getting the funds to the orphanage had become problematic. As the memorial fund grew, we began making inquires. The first thing we learned was that our well-intentioned fundraising efforts had brought attention to the orphanage, an orphanage run by Catholic nuns in a Muslim city with a mission of quietly retrieving children who had been abandoned because of their physical deformities. There were extremists in the city who would resent both the Christian presence and the public revelation of the fact that these children had been abandoned in the first place. It was possible that the publicity would cause the nuns to be forced out or, worse yet, get them killed.

We stopped talking publicly about the orphanage and prayed that our ignorance would not bring harm to the sisters, but one persistent reporter wanted to do a follow-up story. Our reluctance to talk about the fund or how much money it had raised seemed to fuel his determination to investigate and write about it. Most journalists quickly understood the reasons we needed to let the story die, but I couldn't seem to get though to this particular young man, and I finally appealed to his editor, explaining that lives were literally at stake. In the months that followed, a car-bomb was detonated in front of the orphanage. All the windows were shattered, but by the grace of God, no one was hurt.

At the outset, we had given no thought to how we would get the money to the orphanage; we assumed we would do some research, find their website, get an address, and send them a check. But there was no website. In fact, I found several notices, on the websites of well-meaning organizations, explaining that they had been asked to remove any information that might facilitate making donations to the Missionaries of Charity, the order that ran the Baghdad Orphanage. You could find references and articles, but no easy way to give money. As we continued to gather information, we learned that the order, founded by Mother Teresa, did no fundraising. They believe that since they were doing God's work, He would meet their needs, daily, that there was no need to stockpile money or raise funds.

The nuns ushered us into a simply furnished room with a table and chairs. The entire family filed in accompanied by Joan, our former media spokesperson, who lived in Minnesota. Sister Nirmala, who had taken up the mantle of Mother Teresa after her passing, was visiting mission sites around the world. When we learned that she would be in Minneapolis, we asked if we could meet with her. We had no idea how it would play out. We assumed that we would introduce ourselves, tell our story, and ask how the money should be conveyed, a process that would require no more than ten minutes. Even that seemed like a lot to ask of a woman who was responsible for a worldwide order that had over 4500 members in 133 countries.

She was dressed in a simple white habit, trimmed in blue, but when this tiny woman entered the room her presence seemed to fill it. She sat quietly for a moment, and then, after we introduced ourselves, she made us feel as though there was nothing else on her agenda.

We explained how Michelle had been a soldier in Iraq and how she had visited the Baghdad Orphanage. We gave her a copy of the letter Michelle had written about the experience, and to my surprise, Sister Nirmala read it as we sat there. She began to comfort us, assuring us that Michelle was in God's care now, and then she spent the next thirty minutes telling us stories of both miraculous protection and heartbreaking loss among the sisters of the order. Somewhere during this time, in another room, the nuns began their litany, the daily singing of prayers and we sat, enthralled, as she told us her stories to the nuns' serenade.

She told us about a mission in some impoverished island nation. A storm surge had sent flood waters into the village, and the nuns watched as a Volkswagen bus that had been donated to the order was lifted up by the flood waters and carried out to sea. The nuns cried out to God, reminding him that the van was an essential part of their work, and after a time, they saw the van reverse direction as the flood waters carried it back to their doorstep. Not all the stories were happy ones.

They had recently lost two sisters to political violence after they had chosen to stay with their mission rather than flee the country after a revolution had begun.

Before we left, Sister Nirmala gave us each prayer cards and necklaces containing the image of Mother Theresa and posed for pictures with us. Then she gave us the name of someone in her organization that could help us make arrangements to transfer the funds. As we finished, I could feel what Michelle felt, what she wrote about in the letter, a transcendent peace that seemed to flow from an encounter with these extraordinary women.

Journal Entry – *November 2004*

Sign Language

My heart does not have the power of speech. It simply sends feelings to my brain, which I must try to interpret and translate into words and coherent thoughts. But my heart is often more perceptive than my brain, sensing things long before my brain becomes aware of them. Even so, I cannot allow my heart to take charge, especially now. If my heart had its way, I would do nothing but think of her, do nothing but curl up in a rocking chair and feel my grief. It's my brain that gets things done. It's my brain that goes to work in the morning and manages projects and makes executive decisions and keeps the pain at a distance.

The trouble started the Wednesday before Thanksgiving. I had spent the last two weeks working very hard on a project at work and I had paid little attention to my heart. I was ignoring it on purpose. I didn't have time to tend to its ups and downs or pander its moodiness. Since Michelle died, my heart has been difficult and unpredictable. The meltdown occurred when I was getting ready for work in the morning, listening to the radio. The show presented a mother of a fallen soldier who told the story of how her son was killed only days before he was scheduled to come home. When the mother told of how she had circled her son's homecoming date on every calendar in the house, my heart took control of me and I began to cry, and cry hard.

Every attempt to reason with it was fruitless. I reminded my heart that we were short-staffed at work, that there was an important project that needed my attention. No change; the crying continued. I watched the minutes on the clock tick by and fretted as my schedule went out the window. I began to bargain: we don't have to get to work early; we can take a little more time. If I could get my heart under control and still get to work on time, I might be able to get some things done before the phone started ringing.

I try to console my heart: "Yes, this will be a difficult time, the holiday season, that's to be expected, let's just take it one day at a time ..." I was making no progress; I wasn't getting through. I began to realize there was more to it. It wasn't about facing Thanksgiving or Christmas without her. In its feeble way, my heart finally began to make me understand. How could I have missed it? The way this day looked, the gray morning, the way the winter light came through the windows. It was a year ago. It was one year ago when they came home on leave, when Rachel and Michelle came home for fifteen glorious days. For fifteen days, we had been a family again. It was an oasis in the desert of anxiety where we wandered in during their deployment.

It was one year ago that I hugged her for the last time, hugged my Michelle, in the airport, for the very last time. Watched her walk down the concourse until I couldn't see her anymore, waving to her, hoping she would look back just one last time.

My heart wouldn't let me forget this anniversary. It made me remember.

Chapter 23 - Five

Journal Entry – December 2004

Christmas

It's Christmas Eve. I'm sitting in my recliner with my laptop. Buster, my dog, is lying beside me, looking like a badly worn black shag carpet. He's dozing and occasionally he snores. Lori is in the kitchen preparing food for later, when the kids drop by. The TV is set on the Family Channel and neither of us is paying attention to the made-for-TV movie chattering away in the background.

Christmas is here. It is both worse than we thought it would be and not as bad as we thought it would be. We mix pockets of "normalcy" with streaks of coming completely undone. We have wandered down aisles of the grocery store, crying because something triggered a memory and started us thinking about how much we miss Michelle. We get lost in gift shopping, but at some point we are jolted by the fact that we are buying for one less person, that there is one less stocking hanging from the mantle.

My extended family traditionally gathers on Christmas Eve. My brothers and sisters living in this part of the country take turns hosting the event. It should have been our turn this year. But my sister wisely took the pressure off by offering to host the gathering. All we have to do was muster the energy to show up. We didn't know if we would make it until we are actually in the car, driving to the party.

Although I have never had to deal with cancer, I believe there are some similarities between the grieving process and battling cancer. Cancer survivors often have to endure chemotherapy. Ironically, the very chemotherapy that can save their lives can make them temporarily sicker. Family gatherings are like that for me. I know my family's love is a healing force. But gathering with them over the holidays reinforces the loss, emphasizes the fact that Michelle is missing. This makes me temporarily sicker.

We make it to the party. We eat appetizers, sample cookies, and drink punch. We take pictures, catch up on family news, and have our traditional "white-elephant" gift exchange. I feel both the pain of loss and the joy of family. And in the end, I know that I am better off for coming. I know that this "chemo" is healing me.

Journal Entry – *January 2005*

Five

This time, I am getting my hair cut. The stylist is making conversation, talking about her daughter, commenting on how every time she turns around, there's another school expense to deal with. "It's so expensive to raise children now days," she complains. Then she asks the question, the one I have struggled with over the last nine months: "Do you have any children?"

"Yes," I reply, and leave it that.

"How many?" she prods.

The first time this question came up was just a few weeks after Michelle was killed. I was in church. At the end of the service, the pastor encouraged us "to greet someone" on our way out. I talked briefly with the woman seated next to me. "Do you have any children?" she inquired. I stumbled over the words as I answered, "I have four children—well actually, I had five children—I have four *surviving* children—one has passed away." Saying it felt awkward. No matter how I answered the question, it felt wrong. Saying I had four children seemed disrespectful to Michelle. Saying I had five children seemed like a half-truth. Trying to explain seemed like I was fishing for pity.

After this experience, I was determined to figure this out, to figure out how to answer this question and to be prepared for it the next time I was asked. The answer didn't come in a flash. Over the weeks and months, it grew in me until one day I was simply aware of this truth: I have five children. I will always have five children. The fact that Michelle has died does not change the fact that she is my child and will always be my child. She lives on, and one day we will be together again.

The hair stylist's question does not cause my breath to catch or my palms to sweat because I know the answer. How could I have ever answered any differently?

"I have five children."

Journal Entry – January 2005

Searching Behavior

I had never heard the song as part of a regular worship service. When I heard the lyrics, "There is a candle ..." rise up from the platform to the balcony where I was sitting, I panicked. Who would understand if I broke down and cried after only a few words of a song?

The last time I heard "Go Light Your World" was at Michelle's memorial service. It was the closing song, and I was unprepared to hear it again. I struggled to regain my composure and for a moment I convinced myself that I could get through it. Then I told myself that I just needed to leave the sanctuary long enough to straighten up. I went into the hallway, but I never went back. Instead, I used the fire exit to leave the building, trudging through the snow to the parking lot because this option seemed better than having to explain to anyone why I was crying.

I went home and tried to go about my business, but everything got to me. I turned on the TV only to turn it off when I couldn't deal with the show's sad plotline. I got in the car to run errands but instead ended up driving aimlessly. I turned on the radio to listen to *A Prairie Home Companion*, hoping the show's humor would cheer me up. But the show's musical guests performed a haunting operatic duet and I started to cry.

I ended up at the cemetery. I told myself I just wanted to make sure the Christmas wreath was still in good condition—that I was just going to drive by. I had no intention of walking two-hundred yards through the deep snow to Michelle's grave. But when I got there, I found a path had been plowed. I puzzled over this as I walked to her headstone until I got closer and realized that there had been a recent interment in the same area of the cemetery.

There I was, once again, standing in front of her headstone. I tell myself that I come here because I want to keep flowers on her grave, so that everyone will know how much we love and miss her. But there's more to it. I come here because there is a part of me that still hasn't accepted what has happened, that still can't believe there is a grave to visit. There is a part of me that comes to the cemetery hoping that, this time, Michelle's headstone will not be among the thousands of identical white markers—that I will walk to the spot and find that there has been a mistake—that none of this is real.

Journal Entry – February 2005

The Dream

I lay in bed feeling sad. A wave of grief washed over me, and I thought hard about how much I missed her, how much I wanted to see her. I concentrated on seeing her face in my mind, as if by doing so I could somehow bring her back. I tossed and turned and finally fell asleep.

In the dream, she is with me, she is talking to me. Like most dreams, most of it doesn't make sense, but two events register. We are sitting at a computer, apparently reviewing an online bank record. Michelle is talking to me about her finances. She is dressed in her desert BDUs. She tells me that she wants to make sure all of her paychecks get deposited into her savings account.

Then she introduces me to two little girls. The two little girls are Michelle and Charity. They are six or seven years old. For a moment, I am standing between six-year-old Michelle and twenty-year-old Michelle. She seems to know how precious this is to me, and she makes it clear that she has somehow made this amazing thing possible. The little twins are all smiles, dressed in colorful clothes with their hair done in pigtails.

I am struck by the fact that I am talking to her. We do not acknowledge the fact that she is dead. We just share and talk and smile.

I went to bed deeply missing her, but then there she was in my dream, like an answer to a prayer. When I wake up, I am at once happy and sad; happy that I had this brief reunion, sad because it vanished with the night.

This is the first time I've dreamed of my Michelle since I lost her ten months ago.

Journal Entry – March 2005

The Meeting

The coffee is instant. You stir it into a Styrofoam cup with a plastic spoon. The cookies are neatly arranged on a paper plate, next to the hot water. It's the kind of meeting room you find in most any church. We are seated around a long table. There's room for at least thirty people. It's seven-thirty, time for the meeting to start, and less than half the chairs are filled. Later, most the seats will be taken, but the meeting never starts on time because people drift in late. I speculate that this is because many of the attendees go through the same mental tug of war I do, trying to decide whether to make the effort to come to the meeting.

Some of the people around the table are regulars. They've been coming for years. The first few times I came to the meetings, I didn't understand this. It seemed pathetic. I certainly didn't want to think of myself coming here three, five, or ten years from now. After a few months, I realized that the veterans come not so much for themselves but to support the new arrivals.

The meeting is called to order. The facilitator is soft-spoken and shares leadership with another woman. They briefly explain what brought them to this group. One lost a son in a motorcycle accident, the other in a car accident. We go around the table, each giving the name of the child we lost and briefly describing our families. Then we take a moment to recognize February birthdays. I light a candle for Michelle.

"Tonight's topic is 'anger,'" explains the facilitator. She is so soft-spoken it's hard to imagine her ever having an angry moment. She explains that anger is part of the grieving process. Later she describes the anger she felt when the police officers at the scene of the accident would not allow her to see her son.

She asks a few open-ended questions and, slowly, the group begins to volunteer its experiences. At first, the comments are punctuated with long periods of silence, but as the night goes on, the discussion becomes more fluid, more conversational.

I spend a lot of the time looking at my feet. I begin to realize how emotionally numb I am and I share this observation with the group.

I listen to a mother who lost a son just two months ago talk about her frustration with the behavior of some of her family members, at the funeral. This jars loose some of my own unpleasant memories, and I realize that it's a short trip from numb to angry.

They gather the last Monday of every month. They gather to do their "grief work." The theory is that in order to heal, we must actively and consciously work through the swirl of emotion and confusion that surrounds the loss of a loved one. It's not fun. It's like physical therapy: you know it's going to hurt, but you do it because you believe that in the long run, it will make you feel better.

Journal Entry – April 2005

The Bubble

The outside air is thin, filled with uncertainty and mystery; life is fragile in its presence. Inside, we breathe easy and our lives are filled with busyness and routine, consistent and stable as far as the eye can see. I've written about the bubble before. It's the way I describe the "normal" we create for ourselves. We all do it; we need "normal" to function in this world. Normal is like a space helmet that allows us to breathe in a hostile environment.

Losing someone dear to us breaks the bubble and we gasp for air as we are confronted with all of life's big questions, the chief among them being, "Why? Part of the healing process is reconstructing the bubble. In my experience, the bubble collapses many times during the process. The longer it stays in place, the stronger it becomes, the harder it is to break.

It is said that you never get over the loss of a loved one; instead you learn to incorporate that loss in to a "new normal." In my case, that means the bubble will always have a small hole in it, just large enough to let through some mystery, some uncertainty, some pain. This hole will keep me connected, always, to my Michelle, like a limp connects you to the injury that caused it.

In the dream, I am about to run a race. There's a festive atmosphere, a large crowd is milling about. My older brother, Joe, appears out of the crowd and says, "John's limping!" Joe appears to be a young man. I have a quick conversation with, Ron, my brother, who is also running the race, and assure him I will be able to run.

I see in the distance, a group of young girls. I recognize Michelle and she recognizes me and waves, eagerly. She looks like she's about thirteen years old. Next, I am moving in a group, a procession along the sidewalk. In a playful way, I sneak up behind Michelle, wrap my arms around her, and say, "I miss you!" Michelle is dressed in a bright yellow shirt. It looks like it's a man's shirt, a buttoned-down oxford. As we begin a conversation, the dream evaporates, and I wake to the sound of Buster, my dog, snoring. I look at the clock and it is precisely four a.m. on Easter Morning. Slowly it dawns on me that I had a dream about Michelle.

I am limping in the dream and I connect that symbol to the journal entry I had written the day before. Then I realize that in my dream, young Michelle is dressed in bright yellow, an Easter color.

She was killed a year ago, on Good Friday. How fitting it is that I would dream of her on Easter morning.

Journal Entry – *June 2005*

49-179A

Daisies last the longest. I usually get the ones that have been dyed a deep red because I think Michelle would like this color and I think they are striking against the smooth white headstone. It's become a ritual. Every weekend, usually on Saturdays, I go to the supermarket and pick out a bouquet of flowers and then drive over to Wood National Cemetery. The grounds are beautiful—green grass, ancient trees, rolling hills, and headstones, thousands of white headstones, lined up like soldiers standing at attention.

I carry a scissors in my car. I keep them in the compartment between the seats. I need them to trim the flowers. There's a bin full of plastic vases. The vases have a spike on the bottom so you can push them into the ground. They come in white and green. I always pick a white vase because I like the way it looks against the headstone. Next to the vases, there is a water barrel, mounted on a stand. A sign warns that the water is not for human consumption. I empty the flower food packet into the vase and fill it with water. Then I stick the vase into the ground and cut the flowers to fit. When I'm satisfied with my work, I pull the vase out of the ground and take the two-hundred-yard walk to Michelle's headstone.

I put flowers on her grave because I want everyone who drives by to know that she was part of a family that loved her. On their way to the veteran's hospital or the baseball stadium, I want them to notice a headstone with a bright bouquet of flowers in front of it and I want them to make the connection. I want them to think about this soldier and all the other soldiers buried in this cemetery. And I want them to understand that these soldiers were once part of a family, a family that loved them, a family that will always miss them, and a family that will never be the same without them.

49-179A is the marker number for Michelle's headstone.

Chapter 24 - A Rose in the Desert

On their last night in town, the commander, of the Company B 118th Medical Battalion arranged for the entire company to assemble and stay at the Marriott Hotel near unit headquarters in Waukesha, Wisconsin. Family members were invited to stay until lights out, so we all squeezed into Charity's room along with a parade of extended family and friends. The room was jammed, which made it all the more noticeable when a tall, dark, and handsome young man braved the crowd and squeezed into the room. Michelle and Rachel's radar seem to detect a spark between Charity and the newcomer and they, along with their mother went on high alert. Within minutes, Charity was lost in conversation with her visitor, and there was no doubt in my mind that Michelle, Rachel, and Lori would insist on a full debriefing at the first possible opportunity.

Tony, the young man who came into the room that night, wore small, wire-rim glasses and a bandana, tied on his head like the GIs you see in war movies. He spoke quietly and thoughtfully, and he seemed to be willing to put up with the crowded, chaotic room in order to spend time with Charity.

Two weeks later, when Charity chose to stay in New York with her unit and her newfound friend rather than come home for Christmas, we knew she was smitten. Granted, there wasn't a strong incentive to come home; Michelle and Rachel would be long gone by Christmas and coming home would have meant another round of "goodbyes" and there was airfare to consider, but still, the choice was significant. The soldiers could choose between going home or going on a USO outing to New York City, which included a Broadway show. I'm not sure if this was the official first date, but after the show, Charity and Tony went to dinner and Charity would tell us later that was the night she knew she was falling in love with him.

Charity corresponded with her sisters, letting them know that the relationship was becoming serious; she was willing to endure the interrogations and teasing she knew this revelation would bring. It was how they looked out for each other, how they kept each other honest.

Early in 2004, Michelle and Tony met, again, on the streets of Baghdad when her convoy was passing near BIAP where Tony, Charity, and the rest of the Company B, 118th Medical Battalion was stationed. Tony recognized Michelle and flagged her down, letting her know that Charity was nearby and steering Michelle toward her twin sister so they could grab a couple minutes together. Although her encounters with Tony were brief, it would give Charity great comfort in the months ahead to know that Michelle had met the man that would become increasingly important in her life.

After Michelle was killed, Tony was there for Charity, corresponding with her daily from his post in Baghdad. They talked on the phone whenever they could, and they even bought headsets that allowed them to talk over the Internet during their year apart. And they wrote each other. Tony was a talented writer, and the letters he wrote to Charity were thoughtful and comforting. Charity wrote back, finding in Tony a safe place to pour out her heart.

Dear Tony,

It's still Sunday night my time and I am just sitting here missing you, so I'd thought I'd write. I need to get it out.

It is my job to make sure I am the one who goes through all of Shelly's things. I know there are things that she wouldn't want anyone else to see or read except me, and I want to make sure I honor that. I know she would have done the same for me. It's hard though; it stirs up emotions I cannot control, nor would I want to for that matter. It is something I need to do. I lock myself in my room and slowly, piece by piece, go through every letter, every note that she has kept, that somehow had significance in her life. I am familiar with every single one. We never kept secrets from each other. I tear through her clothes quickly, and methodically, knowing if I linger on them too long, I won't be able to make it through—and if I can't, no one else will. It is what she would have wanted. I know this in my heart, am sure of it.

I make the piles and am remembering each different occasion where she wore the clothes I am folding. I just can't hold the tears back any longer, knowing she will never wear them again, never shine brilliantly in them as only she could. My heart aches, but I continue to fold, and focus—knowing I must get through this—must force myself to just finish the pile. I am exhausted by the time I am done. I curl up into a ball surrounded by all the things she loved, all the secrets from this world that only I knew about, everything she held dear lying out before me in organized piles. Then I give in and pull her old sweatshirt over my head feeling somehow this will bring me closer to her, bridge the gap between us—Shelly up in heaven, and me down on earth. The door is still locked so I try and muffle my sobs. This is just between me and her. I finally find sleep lying on the floor, dreaming of my beautiful sister, but when I wake she is gone and I remember why I am there, lying on the floor amidst her belongings. And my heart is heavy once again.

I remember the line from the poem by W. S. Merwin and it brings me some comfort:

> It is clear to me that I cannot return
> but that some of us will meet once more
> even here
> like our own statues
> and some of us still later without names
> and some of us will burn with the speed
> of endless departures
>
> and be found and lost no more

I am reminded I will see Michelle again someday and I let out a deep sigh.

Tony, you don't know what your words mean to me, how I read them over and over, how much they strengthen me, how I know you are with me, can feel you through the distance. I love you so much. Please never stop loving me.

~ Charity

In July 2004, Tony's mother, Nancy, invited Charity, Rachel, and Lori to Lunch. Midway through the meal, Nancy's phone rang and Charity was surprised to learn it was Tony. Nancy handed Charity the phone, saying that Tony had a question for her and a few seconds later Nancy produced a small ring box.

With an ocean separating them, Tony proposed to Charity, reading her a poem and then asking her to spend the rest of her life with him. Charity said "Yes." And with that yes our families, The Witmers and the Verres, had been given a new mission: we had a wedding to plan. And we vowed it would be a wedding to remember.

I was not surprised by the engagement. Tony and I had traded e-mails beforehand. He wanted my blessing. And I was glad to give it to him after I lectured him on how important my Charity was to me and how I needed to be sure he treasured her as much as I did. He did not hesitate or equivocate. His responses to my questions were direct and unwavering, and I felt Charity had fallen in love with the right man.

Chapter 25 - The Homecoming

February 2005

We stood just outside of security on the "E" concourse at Milwaukee's Mitchell Field along with hundreds of other family members, all of us craning our necks, looking for the first sign of soldiers coming through the corridor. There were grandmas and grandpas, moms and dads, children of all ages including babes-in-arms. Some had been born while these soldiers were deployed, so they would be meeting their fathers for the first time.

Foil balloons with "Welcome Home!" and "I Love You" and "Congratulations" hovered above the crowd, and children held long banners that said "We Love you Mom" or "I'm Proud of my Dad." The return of the Company B 118th Medical Unit would be one of the top stories on the ten-o'clock news, and camera crews from all the local stations milled about interviewing family members and getting background stories. We were approached a few times by reporters and asked to talk about our story. But we explained that today the spotlight needed to be on these soldiers and their families.

A shout went up when the first soldier was spotted coming through the security checkpoint. Tears began spilling down the faces of family members who, only now, could fully believe it was over, that their loved one had made it home, that this long year of deployment had finally come to an end and that in just a few minutes they would be embracing their soldier.

Charity and Tony's engagement had been a double-edged sword. The joy was overshadowed by an unspoken fear: what if Tony didn't make it back? What would happen to our daughter if she lost, first, her twin sister and then her fiancé? I don't remember if I ever shared that thought with anyone. It was as if speaking the words would give them power. I'm certain the same thought haunted all of us, but we kept it to ourselves as once again our family waited for a soldier to come home.

We tried to comfort ourselves with the fact that Tony was in a medical unit, but we knew the enemy would often attack what were called "targets of opportunity." This fact was driven home to us in a dramatic way when we learned that the company commander and a small team of soldiers had been seriously injured when a suicide-bomber charged the checkpoint where their convoy had stopped. They escaped death only through the quick thinking of a team member who spotted the bomber and fired on him before he could close the distance between them. Even at a distance, the explosion sent shrapnel tearing through their bodies.

After what seemed like an eternity, Tony walked out of the concourse and in to the arms Charity. Their embrace left little doubt that Sergeant Witmer and Specialist Verre were in violation of the fraternization regulations. The Witmers and the Verres breathed a collective sigh of relief; the wedding was now seven months away, and we would turn our energies toward planning the best party in the history of our families.

On August 20, 2005, our friends and family gathered at Elmbrook Church for Tony and Charity's wedding. The same building we associated with one of the saddest days of our lives became the setting for one of the happiest days of our lives.

Charity was a beautiful bride, and I couldn't hold back the tears when I saw her. Lori and Rachel looked like they had stepped from the pages of a glamour magazine. Rachel sang during the service, and Mark accompanied her on the guitar along with my dear friend Joe Glatzel on the piano. Pastor Scott performed the ceremony, and his words came with the grace and wisdom we had come to expect from this man. The reception was held at the same hotel where I first met Tony, the night before the Company B 118th shipped out, in Charity's room where he had wandered in wearing his bandana and wire-rim glasses.

I have never been happier than I was the night of my daughter's wedding, watching my family celebrate as only those who have know suffering can celebrate. This is the toast I shared at Charity and Tony's wedding:

Solomon, said to be the wisest man that ever lived, wrote this:

To everything there is a season, and a time to every purpose under the heaven:

A time to be born, and a time to die

A time to plant and a time to pluck up that which is planted

A time to kill, and a time to heal

A time to break down and a time to build up

A time to weep, and a time to laugh

A time to mourn and a time to dance

In the past year, our family has known weeping and mourning, but tonight, *tonight* we dance.

We celebrate the fact that, out of the scorched earth of war, a flower sprang up, a rose bloomed, a love was born.

I thank God that Tony and Charity found each other.

I thank God for the *heart* of this young man, Tony, whom I am now privileged to call my son-in-law. He is a kind, sensitive and caring human being.

I thank God for Charity, and I am proud of the woman she has become: Passionate, determined and wise beyond her years.

My prayer for you, Tony and Charity, is this:

May all life's burdens be lighter because you face them together, may all life's joys be fuller, because you have each other.

Tonight we celebrate with you.

And we did; we celebrated with all our hearts and we danced all night long. That's what Michelle would have wanted.

Chapter 26 - Dear Dad

I sat at my laptop that Sunday morning, sipping coffee. It was two years, to the day, since we had lost her. People would be expecting me to put something out on the website to mark the occasion, some sort of update or remembrance. I stared at the keyboard, but the words were not coming. After awhile, my mind started to wander and I wondered what *she* would say to me, about this day, if she could. I picked up my journal, and as I imagined her voice in my head it became so real I began to cry, and as I cried, I wrote.

Dear Dad,

It's been two years and it's time to tell you some things.

I know you will always miss me. I know there is a part of you that will always ache. But it's time for you to embrace the hurt and let it make you stronger.

Dedicate yourself to the people I love. Love them for me. Cherish my brothers and sisters and see my spirit in their smiles. I will always be with you.

People will remember the last minutes of my life, how I died doing my job, at my post, protecting my comrades. They will remember how I loved life. They will remember and they will honor my memory. I left a legacy. Take comfort in this.

You will see me again. I know it's hard to be apart, but my love for you and Mom and Charity and Rachel and Tim and Mark and all my family and friends will always be there. Love is eternal.

Go on, now - go on and use the gifts I've given you.

You will always be compassionate to those who have suffered loss; you will always be sensitive to those who are hurting. You will always remember me, and, doing so, be reminded of the eternal. These are my gifts to you. Use them, and live life well.

I love you forever,

Michelle

I was exhausted by the time I finished writing, but it seemed as real as if she had been speaking to me. I logged on to the website and transcribed the scrawled, barely discernable words from my journal while they were still fresh in my mind. And then I went back to bed and slept hard.

Epilogue - A Letter to Madison

Dear Madison,

Somewhere in your mother's keepsakes is an iPod, engraved with "Merry Christmas from Tony and Benjamin John Verre." The first ultrasound had been inconclusive, but two subsequent ultrasounds brought assurances that you were a boy. The nursery was painted accordingly and the baby shower gifts were purchased with this in mind.

Your mother gave birth to you on January 2, 2007 at about six in the evening. Your Grandma and Rachel were in the room. Rachel was the first one to notice. And when she blurted out, "It's a girl!" the room went quiet. Your mother's voice broke the silence: "Are you sure!" she asked, sounding stunned.

Rachel raced to the waiting room where I sat with Mark and Tim. She burst in and shouted, *"It's a girl!"*

Just like your mother, you made a dramatic entrance into this world. And somehow I knew that Michelle was there laughing with us over this surprise life had handed us.

I tried several times, to start writing these stories; but I never got very far. I couldn't find my voice. But after you were born, things changed. Your birth gave me back something I'd lost. It gave me hope. I couldn't write to the whole world, but I could write to you. I didn't know how to write a book, but I knew that I could write these stories for you. I knew that you would want to know, that you would *need* to know. You would need to know about the pictures of your mom posing with her two sisters, all of them in Army uniforms, about the news videos and clippings I keep in a container in the garage.

And you should know. You should know how they served and what they gave and why they have a place in history. Your mom, your Aunt Rachel, and your Aunt Michelle were soldiers; they were *real* soldiers. It's a story you should know, and when you are ready, this book will be waiting for you.

As I write these words, five years have passed since your Aunt Michelle was killed in action. We've sold the big, old house that drew us to New Berlin, trading it for a townhouse just a block off of Michelle Witmer Memorial Drive. The city named the street after Michelle a year after she died. Your little sister was born six months ago, and now our townhome has Dr. Seuss books and Fisher-Price toys stuffed into shelves and closets on every floor. When you spend time with us, you often point to pictures of Michelle and proudly say "Mommy." We try to explain, but it will be a few more years before you understand it.

Your Aunt Rachel is planning a wedding with your soon-to-be-Uncle Brendan. Brendan is a reporter for one of the local TV stations. He met Rachel after being assigned to do a story on our family when Rachel and Michelle came home on leave in 2003. Michelle tried to do some matchmaking at the time, "He's really good-looking, you should go talk to him!" But Rachel and Brendan did not have their first date until many months after we lost Michelle.

Timothy is only a few classes away from his degree, and he continues to work full time in the IT department of a marketing firm. He bought his own house a few years back, not far from where we live. Mark finished his career in gymnastics, graduated from the University of Minnesota, and decided to make his home in Minneapolis.

Your grandmother is just as active as she's ever been, teaching fitness classes at local clubs and at retirement communities around the area. My day job as an operations manager continues to take me around the country, but I still try to get up early everyday and write a little in my leather-bound journal.

It's important that you understand why your Aunt Michelle's death has a place in history. Yes, she was the first woman to be killed in action in the history of the National Guard, but there's more to it. Michelle's death demonstrated that despite the official prohibition of women in combat, women have stepped out of support roles and are now serving on the frontlines. The night she died, her team was being sent to reinforce a police station under insurgent attack. She was in the gunner turret, the most vulnerable position in the vehicle, manning a

SAW, a machine gun capable of firing 750 rounds per minute. This country may not be ready to hear that, but she was one of many female soldiers in this war who gave their lives this way. I believe that historians will look back at the Iraq-Afghanistan war as a time of profound change in the role of women in the military.

After Michelle's death, Specialist Shizuko Jackson, one of Michelle's closest friends, wrote these words about her:

> She should be remembered for giving her own money, clothes she found, and toys to poor children near our police station. ... The children *loved* Michelle, and they literally chanted her name every time we pulled up to the station, "Michelle! Michelle! Michelle!" Months later, after we left Al-Quanat for another mission, whenever we came back to visit, the kids still remembered her and asked for her "Where is MY Michelle?!!" That's what she should be remembered for.

I ask you to remember your Aunt Michelle. Remember a young woman who could find something to be thankful for even in a war zone. Remember a young woman who brought comfort not only to her fellow soldiers but to the people of Iraq. Remember a young woman who embodied both the strength of a soldier and the heart of an angel.

Love you forever,

Grandpa